HIGH-RISE

OBSERVATIONS AND SECRETS OF A DOORMAN

A. B. C. DELEVANTE

PAGE PUBLISHING, INC.
New York, NY

First originally published by Page Publishing, Inc. 2018

ISBN 978-1-64350-851-1 (Paperback)
ISBN 978-1-64350-852-8 (Digital)

Printed in the United States of America

To my mother
M. W.
a gentle soul who came into this world
and demanded nothing

We love the truth when it reveals itself,
But hate the truth when it reveals ourselves.

—St. Augustine.

We must live together as brothers, or perish together as fools.

—Martin Luther King Jr.

CONTENTS

AUTHOR'S NOTE

Upon reading this book, the reader may come to his or her own conclusion on the individuals in the book which best personifies each of these titles.

CHARACTERS DEPICTED IN THIS BOOK

The Lonely
The Fearful
The Bewildered
The Vampires and Monsters
The Angels and Saints
The Simple
The Gossipers
The Old
The Young
The Anti Semites
The Hypocrites
The Dreamers

What good is there? Pray thee, tell me in jostling through the crowd in life amid the argumental tumult, protestations and endless strife, mole like, borrowing in darkness grasping for the spider's thread always thwarted in ambition, until the living joins the dead.

—Khalil Gibran

PREFACE

How true it is, that if you gaze intensely at a face (including your own), you will then see the humanity of the individual? You will see in that individual's face the character of humankind, our fears, our fleeting moments of glee, our pains, our fragility, our strengths, and in some cases, a degree of innocence. You will also see in our faces our mortality, that mysterious mark of death which lurks behind each and every moment of life.

Faces can also be masks, which attempt to hide the true inner and outer countenance of the wearer, but by looking intently and intensely for a longer period, one can eventually penetrate this mask to unveil thoughts, aspirations, disappointments, expectations, and frailty hiding in shadowy corners.

It is also true that doormen are likened to bartenders and psychologists, to whom people come to spill their guts. In some instances, one can hear an entire life story in (believe it or not) fifteen minutes. If it's not a life story, it could also be significant life-changing events, or on the other hand, sometimes just insignificant prattling.

A doorman not only open doors for the residents and their guests. He also acts as a mentor (and in some ways) counselor, psychologist, listener, and comforter.

Doormen opens doors for others while others open their hearts, their worries, their pains, their secrets, and their lives to the doormen.

THE LONELY

High-rises consist of individuals with almost every type of characteristics which are to be found in all of us—vampires, monsters, hypocrites, saint, angels, every who in whoville, and also some very lonely people.

It is the lonely for which more sympathy should be felt because, in most cases, they don't even realize that they are lonely.

Loneliness, from my observations in this high-rise complex, is not the goal to be popular, not the wanting to be noticed, not the desire for companionship, not the longing for a mate or lover. It is the need to find a listener.

True listeners are endangered. To be a listener, the virtues of tolerance, patience, and understanding needs to be exercised always. A person who will listen and absorb all which is directed into their ears and minds in turn provides some degree of comfort to the teller.

As we all may be aware, loneliness manifests itself in many forms.

One can feel lonely in a crowd numbering thousands, even millions, simply because the individual does not feel connected to anyone or anything there. Also, no one there talks to or tries to make any type of gesture or connection with this individual.

Loneliness sometimes comes when people distance themselves from each other due to domestic, religious, psychological, financial, and other reasons such as abandonment or death of a significant other or others.

Another unsuspecting contributor to our loneliness is our addiction to electronic devices, namely, computers, cellular phones, and the like.

Despite offering a form of communication that travels through cyberspace in seconds, social media and other forms of electronic socialization are somewhat impersonal. The lack of interpersonal contact slowly and eventually deprives us of one of our most basic privilege or need: the human-to-human contact, the simple act of looking into a person's eyes as you shake their hand, touching a hand, a hug or an embrace during times when consolation is needed. The simple things that make us human, the things that bind us are quietly disappearing, silently losing ground in our relentless pursuit of artificial intelligence and convenience.

I came to realize that some of the lonely in this High-rise are people who lacks self-confidence and use electronic devices as a buffer, which offers a degree of comfort in their interaction with others. While some are individuals who have been scarred by life's unpleasant and unforgiving chapters.

In this High-rise, and I would imagine many others to be somewhat similar, lived and lives many senior folks of which some are the sweetest souls you can imagine, but the majority are truly miserable souls. Of this majority, most are women who (as a male resident puts it) have nagged their husbands to death and are now looking for a new prey. These women (and some men also) are the monsters and vampires of this High-rise. They seek out problems even where and when it doesn't exist. They nitpick everything, and if they cannot find any problems, they create it in their heads, and whatever the problem is or whether it's real or fabricated, it is always directed at the doormen.

At times the superintendent and the porters get blamed also. But the brunt of the faults, blames, complaints, and dissatisfaction are aimed at the doormen, and not only are the complaints aimed at us, most of the times it is reported that we are the cause of the problems, such as, according to them, looking too grumpy at times, too slow in opening the door, being away from the desk, not announcing guests and delivery persons, residents moving stuff in or out of the building after hours, parking violations, neighbors too noisy, newspaper delivery person did not deliver their paper, and so on.

There are many who have found comfort in the bottle. Some who become busy bodies. They either know or feverishly want to know everyone's business. They want to know who is who, who is that, who is what, who is doing who, and they will go to any length to get the scoop, then gossip takes over and spreads like a California wildfire, and because they think that the doormen see and knows all the happenings, they see us the prime source for information.

Fortunately for them, there is one doorman in this high-rise who delivers. We call him the Mouth.

The pool deck for the busybodies is one of their favorite hangouts. The old biddies will gather in groups of three to five either sitting in lounge chairs wearing swimsuits that reveal withered arms and legs that complement features on their faces, which reflect the faces of the years. Each wrinkle or crease acts like a notch for each year of their existence on God's green earth.

If you should listen closely, you would hear each of these little groups whispering and gossiping about everyone and each other.

Helen, an older lady who is also a resident, is quite often the subject of many of their gossip gatherings. She is someone one would refer to as a cool old lady. Despite being in their age group, she does not hang out with them.

Helen will often jokingly say, "I don't like to hang out with old people," then she would smile. Even though being an older person, she can most often be seen in the company of people half or sometimes less than half her age. She says this makes her feel younger, which (according to her) is good for her ego and her mental stability.

Helen also has something that the other older folks don't have: Helen is young at heart. Though she is fully aware of and accepts her age, she does not dwell on it, as the others do. She tries to stay younger in her mind and body as much as she can. Therefore (as she puts it), she is spared the aches and pains.

Helen is also the envy of the other girls, because she has a boyfriend and has changed a few of them over the past couple of years. All of them a few years younger than her, spry-looking older gentleman/ guys who thinks and acts just like her.

When asked when she will eventually settle down with one, she replied, "I just have to keep doing this until I get it right." Meaning, keep trying different ones until she finds someone who will, or close to it as possible, fill the void left when her husband left her and ran off with a younger woman.

The other gossiping woman swears that she is doing this as a form of revenge to appease herself. Helen is fully aware that she is the talk of the other ladies and that she is one of their main gossip topics, but she swears that they are just plain jealous, so when asked if it bothers her, quite often her response would be "BFD" and when asked the meaning of it, she replies, "Big fucking deal."

Helen's pal Nina, a lady in her mid-seventies who shares similar mind-set and often stops at the desk to chitchat, as she did one day when, while chit chatting, she said, "Oh, I went to my appointment today to my gynecologist, and he told me that I have a vagina like a sixteen-year-old."

OBSERVATIONS

Being a doorman working in a high-rise and stationed at the front desk means you are highly visible to the residents and their guests and those employed by the residents. During any given shift, many people will come and go, passing through the lobby. Some would be upbeat, jovial, and friendly. Then there are others who are not friendly, but will display little manners by saying "good morning," "good evening," or good day." Others will want to walk in with their heads held straight without a passing glance. They will want to pass us, as if we are invisible. The latter is usually done by people of a certain decent. We interpret this behavior to be a practice of their culture and way of life, where they look down on people based on the work they do, but we have our way of telling them, "You're in America now. We do not recognize that crap over here." So we stop them in their tracks and inform them that in order to get past us, they first have to acknowledge us by declaring who they are by signing in then tell us where they would like to go or the person they are visiting. In the case of residents or owners who are from the same culture, we try to tolerate and ignore this behavior, and if we happen to see them in another setting, like in a store or on a sidewalk, we would give them the same treatment, a dose of their own medicine.

If there is one thing we know for certain, it's that we, the doormen, are thoroughly scrutinized, watched, and discussed by the residents, among themselves as well as with their families and guests. We can only imagine the negative, indifferent, and hopefully a little bit of good that is being said about us. We firmly believe that most of the comments about us are negative, even though we try our very best to serve, cater to, and accommodate the residents and their guests in every way possible.

Despite all the negative rumors being propagated about the doormen in this high-rise. There are a number of genuinely good, positive, and respectful people living here.

The good ones are mostly quiet, calm, and friendly. The complete opposite of the nitpickers, the restless, and the fabricators who dedicate a significant amount of their time to digging up insignificant old bones, long buried and forgotten, every day conducting their own ill-informed audit of the finances of the building or constantly searching for whatever they can come up with to blame on the staff.

In the eyes of these individuals, nothing is ever done right in the building, and all decisions made by the board of directors for improvements to the building were poorly made, because they were not consulted for their input. Absolutely nothing pleases or satisfies these people, yet they are totally appeased by rumors, gossips, and bad news, even when the bad news is false.

This is not a book about a story, or a book about one event, or showing events in the life of an individual, or events in the lives of a few individuals, but rather events about multiple lives in a hi-rise complex.

A complex of lives engaged in the game of survival, the game of life with all its twisted complexities, it's moments of joy, sadness, sorrows, and confusion—reflections of all of us.

I write with the notion that the individuals mentioned here, in this volume, can be found in the people around us, the ones we interact with every day, in our buildings, churches, schools, neighborhoods, and communities.

This lowly or humble position as doorman, in reality is, in the true sense of the term, "the classic dead-end job" that commands no respect and no room for growth.

If there is anything this job has to offer, it would be the chance to listen and try to understand the human psyche and to get a pension. In this job as doorman, we see the dying, the bigots, the dreamers, the cheaters, the alcoholics, the hypocrites, the sick, the weak, the good, the bad, the humble, the monsters, the vampires, the saints, and the angels, just to mention a few.

Stationed at the front desk, we get to see all. We see the brides being ushered out on their way to the altar to become wives. We see the timid grooms passing through with the look of uncertainty hiding behind forced smiles.

We watched in silence over the years as ambulances pulled up to take the sick and dying out of their sanctuaries. We see the faces of the happy parents with their newborns returning from the hospitals. We watch these babies as they grow into gleeful youngsters. We see when the repo man comes to take the residents' cars and the confrontations that at times ensued.

In this high-rise, we see the ones with no gentlemen or ladies calling and, with nary a visitor, have found content in living alone. On the flip side, we observe others who crave attention, to the point where they will have several callers per week. These are the ones looking for Mr. or Ms. Right. At times, there can be more than one caller in a single day. We know this because there are times when the caller in the apartment at that time either overstays or gets carried away with or in whatever they were engaged in, the resident will call us, saying, "Please tell my visitor to wait there in the lobby for a few minutes." Fifteen minutes later, the phone rings. "Send the person up, please," but we know that the one who had just left was hastily hurried out the side door. We have seen this and similar situations played out over and over, and rarely has it ever resulted in finding Mr. or Ms. Right, but they keep on trying, hoping that someday, they will get it right. Because as the saying goes, "At times on the brink of success, we all have the tendency to give up or quit."

It is something that befall the vast majority of us, I am not sure if I should call it procrastination or perhaps taking time for granted. In fact, we all fall victim to it to some degree, and at points in our lives, it becomes our nemesis.

In this High-rise, I have seen it over and over again in various highly intelligent people, who when at the lobby front desk or round table would sometimes, briefly talk about things they want to accomplish, places they want to see or relocate to, uncompleted projects they truly would love to complete, and so on.

And as life hurries by, these wishes, hopes, and desires get put off for next week, next month, next year, and next year turns into years and years, then suddenly, they stop in their tracks, saying to themselves, "My god, I can't believe that ten years has passed so quickly. I can't believe the neighbor's kid is now going off to college. It's hard to believe the song I'm humming was recorded twenty-five years ago, and to top it off, I find it difficult to accept the appearance of the image staring back at me when I look in the mirror then alas! "Tristfully, as they lay, either weak without the strength of yester-years, cognizant of the stark reality that they can't go back, they've lost time, lost ground, lost themselves trying to navigate their way through the maze, which we call organized society, with all of its laws, rules, and expectations.

As time marches on, so does life, which is made up of time, but unfortunately, unlike time, individual life fades with time's relentless march, which finds many of us on our deathbeds angry with our-selves and filled with regrets for things we wanted to do, things we should have done, things we started and abandoned, and things we kept putting off for tomorrow.

In this high-rise, I have seen far too many of these regretful indi-viduals bedridden, or with two constant companions—their nurse's aides and their walkers or wheelchairs. These once-strong, active, and feisty individuals lay there in their units defecating and wetting on themselves. On occasions when trying to walk, they would fall, so very often the doorman gets the call to come up and help with pick-ing them up. Ninety-nine percent of the time we made no attempt to pick them up; instead, we prefer to call the paramedics for them to handle that type of situation.

While awaiting the arrival of the paramedics were some of the times when we would hear many poignant remarks. Laying there on the floor, they would look up at us, saying, "Look at me, look at what I have become. I used to be strong and able. There are so many things I wanted to do and should have done, so many ideas, so many plans, and look at me now. I thought I had all the time in the world to do everything, and even with the awareness that life is short and time flies, it crept up on me like a thief in a dark night. Now I am useless and hopeless."

The tendency to take time for granted does not describe the few among us. For the most part we are all guilty of it in many ways.

In the event of their deaths, quite often, the children and relatives of these individuals are also ridden with guilt, saying to themselves and revealing to us (the doormen) that while a parent or relative was alive, they could have and should have spent more time engaging them. They should have listened more, should have expressed more, should have done more for them.

I'm sure that many of us can relate to this feeling of guilt when a loved one is no longer with us, this feeling that we failed. We fell short when it came to giving of ourselves.

I will always remember the words of my dear grandmother, when she would say to us, "You will be once a man and twice a child." If you will be blessed or privileged with old age, so in your younger and stronger years, do not forsake the elderly and the weak, because someday you may become one of them.

In the years spent, stationed at the front desk, I have observed many elderly people who have lived and died in the hi-rise. These people spent most of their years wholly attached to their apartments and have, at times, expressed that they would have liked to move on, to see what other cards life would have dealt them, what other possibilities might have awaited, and maybe a little adventure, but they became so hopelessly attached to their places of dwelling, their surroundings, their way of life, and as time marches on and the forerunners fade and die, I observe others, newcomers, falling in line, treading the same path. Much like the rest of us, with the exception of the few, in life, we find a spot and settle into it, and getting out becomes a mental battle or challenge, and the term *homeowner* may need to be rephrased because, with all of the care and maintenance and pampering the property requires, and not to mention the time spent attending to the mortgage, it would be fitting to say that the property owns us, instead of the other way around.

What it boils down to is, if there is a lesson to be learned by us all, it may be found in a certain holy book, in a statement written by one of that book's wisest contributors, the statement reads, "Whatsoever thy hand findeth to do, do it with thy might; for there is no work nor device, no knowledge or wisdom, in the grave whither thou goest."

To find oneself stuck in any situation on the winding road of life, and though the struggle to get out can sometimes seem futile or impossible, like an unsuspecting insect caught in the spider's web, like that insect, we should never stop trying to free ourselves from whatever holds us back even if it means fighting to the very end. Unlike the insect, we have complex brains capable of finding creative ways of freeing ourselves from life's snares.

As the writer of this brief outlook on some of the situations, events, surprises, and things I have observed in this hi-rise, and life in general, I too have had to put up gallant struggles and fights, in order to free myself from those snares. We all may agree that all honest work is honorable, but the dead-end job or position of a doorman could become somewhat of a sinkhole, which may require a bit of personal struggle to climb out of.

After graduating art school and trying teaching for a few years, fate and curiosity brought me to the position as doorman, and almost any doorman will tell you that once in, it takes hold and consumes us. Maybe we are stuck because of the paycheck. Although small, unfortunately, many in our ill-fated line of work depends on it. Is it the routine that we have become so used to? The fear that if we seek change, it will disrupt our false sense of comfort?

Yet in a strange paradox, in the back of our minds, there lingers the hope that something big will happen to bring about that change. I cannot count the many times I've listened to my fellow doorman uttering, "If I could only just win the lottery or come into some money, someway, someday, I would get the hell out of here so fast, so fast ..."

Year after year, I've made solemn promises to myself, that each would be my last stationed at this hi-rise lobby, front desk, playing multiple roles in that lowly position, like a one-man band playing all the instruments, hoping, as he plays, that his audience will be pleased with his performance and his efforts.

I can't pinpoint what has kept my counterparts tied to the job, but speaking for myself, I can say, maybe it's the intrigue in engaging the variety of personalities each day. Maybe it's the satisfaction and sense of purpose gained from helping the elderly and disabled get to and from the vehicles stopped at the front, dropping them off or picking them up. Maybe it's the lessons and things learned from the conversations with the enlightened residents. Maybe it's the inspiration of the old-timers who would often tell their tales of yesteryears. Maybe it's the humor of the jolly old men, telling dirty or corny jokes. Maybe it's the quiet chuckle I get when the know-it-alls have left after making their rounds at the front desk or round table unloading their news of the day and their take on current affairs, along with their expertise on political matters. Maybe it's the innocent, unbiased smiles of the toddlers and infants, the children of residents who have gotten so used to us that they are always eager to come to the lobby to see, smile, and wave to us. Maybe it's all of the above that kept me stuck in this hard-to-like position. Much like the vast majority who dread the reality of getting up and out each day to begin the ritualistic cycle or routine of getting to jobs they despise to the point of hate, but are compelled to do in order to survive in our organized society, where money is king, and unfortunately in our modern system, we trade our most precious commodity—time (the invisible entity of which life is made of) in pursuit of this king, which can play two major roles in our lives—a welcome blessed savior or the root of all evil.

Fortunate are those who truly enjoy their jobs; for the rest of us who don't, what we call a job is in reality the stealer of our precious time, the stealer of our lives.

Of all the contributing factors that could keep one doing a job of this nature, unawarely stuck, the meeting and getting to know (sometimes very in-depth) the different characters and the personalities behind them is perhaps the most interesting as well as the most unexpected. Interesting because, if one has the patience to be a good listener, there is no limit to the things one can or could learn.

Unexpected because, no matter how much you think you know about the characteristics, thinking, and behaviors of humankind, if you listen and observe more keenly, you will become aware that you haven't even begun to learn the alphabet of the behaviors, thoughts, and capabilities of the human animal.

The mere act of listening, talking to, and mingling with many individuals from different backgrounds, different cultures, and different mind-sets—the job as doorman offers some degree of insight into the fabric of our being.

Presented here are a few of the numerous individuals I've either encountered or gotten to know in this very eventful high-rise.

DEXTER

In the case of Dexter, a forerunner in this complex, he is a person who others would refer to as either strange, odd, off the wall, flaky, or just plain nuts. At any given time, he would wander into the lobby (the lobby desk or round table is likened to a psychologist's office, a confession chamber, etc., all wrapped up in one spot) to talk about or ask questions that borders somewhere between idiotic and philosophical.

Dexter's tall but overweight figure tells a lot about his diet and lifestyle, with most of the extra weight in his gut. (It is said that the apartment he occupies is likened to a pigsty or hoarder's den with stuff mostly garbage everywhere, the floor littered with already or partially read newspapers most of which are his favorite, *New York Post*). On closer observation, some of these papers are dated as far back as decades ago. Dexi, as I call him, have lived in this high-rise for the past thirty-five plus years and is a loner in every sense of the word. During my twenty-two years in this high-rise working as a doorman, I have not once seen (and a doorman sees almost everything) a single visitor come calling for Dexi.

His car is just the same as his apartment. Filled with unimaginable junk an old and huge American-made car that holds the memories of when these bodacious American-made eight cylinders ruled the American roads and freeways.

He once told me that this car had 750,000 miles and counting, which was a bit hard to believe given the fact that it never had regular maintenance. The body has more dents than a car that had been beaten up by a hailstorm. It has several gray blots or spots, which are remnants of attempted body repairs, yet he boasts about his baby (his car) and how good it has been to him and his parents whom he had lived with for all of his seventy-three years on earth until the day they passed. In short, Dexi has never left home to live on his own.

Despite his snobbish ways, Dexi is a deeply religious guy (a devout Catholic). He speaks about God or his savior with reverence and fear, even though at times he has expressed to me that he can't understand why his Lord and Savior allow so much wicked evil and murderous acts from so many bad people in this world. Whenever Dexi is asked a question he has no answer for or any unexplainable situation, he will tilt his head down while with his finger pointing upward, silently saying, "Only God has the answers."

Dexi, like any true Christian, is always looking for new converts, and a main focus of his is Tiger Woods. He's obsessed about writing and sending a letter to Tiger regarding the golfer's infidelity. He feels deeply, in his own naive, obsessed, fervent way that if Tiger opens up to the Lord about the activities that caused his breakup, then and only then will he (Tiger) start to win tournaments again. So every day that Dexi comes to the lobby, the first thing he would say is "I think I will send a letter to Tiger."

Another person who he has on his radar is a fellow resident and neighbor in this high-rise whose name is Heinrich, who is an atheist to the core and makes no bones about it.

Until the philosophy which holds one race superior and another inferior is finally and permanently discredited and abandoned, until the color of a man's skin is of no more significance than the color of his eyes.

Everywhere is war.

—Haile Selassie 1
(Popularized by Bob Marley in his song "War")

HEINRICH

Heinrich is a seventy-eight-year-old German who will not either confirm nor deny his admiration for the then-Nazi party that was under the rule of their leader, the raving lunatic Hitler.

Heinrich is a complex and complicated hardliner. He believes that a politician who does not perform his duties or a citizen who misbehaves should receive public lashings on their naked ass. He reads and is fascinated by books and documentaries depicting the events of World Wars I and II. He has numerous stories about what he saw as a child growing up during World War II, many tales about seeing people that he knew (storekeepers, neighbors, etc.) that just virtually disappeared. He saw them almost daily and then suddenly or unexpectedly one day they were gone or not there anymore. Then when he asked where they have gone, his mother told him that they were Jews. He relays to me stories of when he saw for the first time the American GIs or soldiers entering his village and how impressed he and others were of their attitude and demeanor. He told of how at times the GIs would throw candies to the kids and they would also give cigarettes to the young ladies or fräulines and then wander off toward and into barns with them for (what he at that time and age did not know) carnal rewards.

He has stories of when (for the first time) he saw black people (in the form of black GIs) and how fascinating and strange it was to see these men or guys with dark complexions or skin and pearly white teeth. In fact, (he said) it was so fascinating and strange that he and his friends, when they saw these men standing and looking down at them as they played in the streets, they all ran away.

Being a person of dark complexion, I responded, saying, "I can't blame you for being startled and running away because if, as kids, we were playing, then looked up and saw a couple of white men (of whom we have never seen the likes of before) glaring down at us, we would also run away from being scared."

Heinrich also thinks (and one can never be completely certain because he sometimes says things that you or I may consider serious) with a smirk on his face, that he is of the super race and that while growing up in the fatherland, the Germans (himself included) would look down on the Italians, the Polish, the Turks, the Russians, and all people from Eastern Europe. He said that Brits were the only ones they had some respect for.

I've often reminded him that on planet Earth, there's only one race—the human race, which comprises of various cultures, customs, beliefs, and skin tones, and that we are merely another species of animal just as frogs, kangaroos, bears, tigers, and all the thousands of other species on Earth, and that all life-forms are interconnected. When it comes to mankind, all human beings on this planet according to Dr. Spencer Wells (the noted geneticist) are descendants of a small group of hunter-gatherers who wandered out of Africa more than 150,000 years ago and populated the earth.

It is no surprise to me that Heinrich scoffs at the findings of Dr. Wells. He holds fast to the idea that he is superior, even though he himself has admitted that the years are now showing on him. He even refers to himself as an old fuck, but his advanced age does not prevent him from at times clicking his heels and giving the Nazi salute.

Heinrich's solution to everything is kill, kill, kill. If Al Qaeda is mentioned his response is "kill the bastards." If it is criminals, "kill the sons of bitches"; bad politicians, "kill the motherfuckers." Let the people fighting civil wars in their countries fight to the end and all kill themselves.

He does not believe in sending aid to any side. Let the starving children all over the world die. No food aid should be sent to them, because when masses of people die, it is nature's way of keeping a check on overpopulation. More than once, during some of the many conversations he and I have had at the lobby desk, his attention would be drawn to people walking their dogs (which are clearly visible due to the huge picture windows and glass doors at this high-rise). The dog walkers carry plastic bags to pick up after their pets have relieved themselves. Heinrich utterly despises these activities. His comment would be "let's shoot the dog."

Oftentimes, after clicking his heels, he would do mock marches around the lobby while humming German marching songs. Despite the odds, Dexi will not give up trying to convert Heinrich. To him religion is a trick, developed by very clever men with the intention to control people. Being a believer in God I once asked him if he believes in the biblical account of Jesus's crucifixion, resurrection, and ascension.

"Rubbish, all rubbish," he replied. Jesus, he explained, was not dead, but only wounded and they, thinking he was dead, placed his body into a cave, and in the middle of the night, he got up and sneaked away.

"And what about the ascension?" I asked. "there was a small crowd who saw him ascend to the heavens."

"Rubbish, utter nonsense," he fired back. Then he explained that Jesus was a smart guy with talents and was able to perform certain magic tricks, so at that point, when it was said that he ascended to heaven was when Jesus performed a little magic trick, and when the people were distracted, he (Jesus) just simply ran into the bushes.

Another of Heinrich's belief is that in order to get anywhere in this society, to be able to move up and ahead, to make something of yourself, and to have leisure time and financial means to "fuck every day and eat six meals a day," you need to be a son of a bitch.

And so the cycle continues where Dexi perpetually pursues Heinrich with the intention of converting him and persuading him to give his soul to the Lord, and Heinrich simply ignoring him, at times calling him a Jesus fanatic while he marches forward headlong to the beat of the Nazi drum, drowning in his own fanaticism.

SHIRLEY

Shirley is a woman of nearly, if not, seventy-eight years old or should I have said seventy-eight years young? Tall, trim, elegant, educated, and cultured, and even though the faces of the years have bestowed upon her some wrinkles and age spots, she hides it well with the careful crafty application of makeup in all forms and at all costs, makeup so carefully applied that when looking at her one cannot accurately guess her true age. She can easily be mistaken for a person twenty years younger. It is easy to see that in her younger years, she was a complete knockout, a physically beautiful woman with stunningly chiseled facial features, which I would liken to the actress Sophia Loren.

Shirley, being fully aware of her younger years and the freshness of youth along with all the compliments received then, is trying with all of her might and with all the tools available to fight off the slow decay of time and the effect it has on her as it does on all of us. If she could only hold back the hands of time, she would do so in a heartbeat.

A corporate woman, she has dedicated her life to her career. She may have been married at some point in her younger years, got divorced, and since then has written men off as no good. She, like several others in this high rise, has no callers and no visitors, but Shirley's case is a bit different, because it seems to me that she does not want visitors. It is as if loneliness had become the essence of her very existence. It had taken over. If at any time she is called via the lobby intercom, she will never answer. Then maybe a half an hour later, she will call the front desk and ask, "Who was that?" She is rarely seen in the common areas of the building. Her unit is her haven, her sanctuary, her world.

She picks up her mail in the wee hours of the night or morning, discards trash at the same time, and when she emerges from her sanctuary, she opens the door only slightly ajar, then stops and freezes to listen for any movement or sound of another person in the hallway, and if there is, she would quickly duck back into her sanctuary and will keep checking until she is certain that the coast is clear.

There have been a few times when she would slip up and is seen by her neighbors who did not recognize her without the makeup on, and in their words, she looked aged beyond her chronological years, and they wondered, is this condition the results of the excessive over-use of the chemicals in the various makeup she applies to her face? Or is this just the fact that time changes everything and these changes are sometimes unfair, unforgiving, and ugly; thus, we come into the world pre-programmed to be vain? And as time slowly twists, turns, shapes, and reshapes our faces, features, and bodies, we devise ways to try desperately to reverse the process, a process that always wins in this tug-of-war.

MRS. STEVENS

Beulah Stevens is truly unique in every way. For a woman of ninety years old, her sleeves are filled with aces. She lives alone like ninety-eight percent of the older ladies in this high-rise. Most of which are rarely visited by their children, grandchildren, or other kinfolks.

To escape the loneliness, most of Beulah's days are spent in the lobby either sitting doing nothing or befriending the doormen while wearing old wrinkled nightgowns. Some are so wrinkled that at times one wonders if she and the nightgowns are competing to see who has the most wrinkles. Half of the time, her hair is undone, as if she had just gotten out of bed, awakened by or from a really bad nightmare. In the lobby, she always wore bed slippers and oversized white socks, which settles in folds at her ankles like mini spare tires that reveal spindly legs that forbids even the memory of muscle tones or fat.

She would hang out in the lobby for no specific reason or purpose. And with all the time spent in the lobby talking, (sometimes incoherently) mumbling, and being nosey, she never revealed anything personal about herself, but one thing which is almost certain is that she is from Worcester, Massachusetts. This is either a fact or she has a strange or compulsive fascination with that city in the great state of Massachusetts, or maybe she just simply likes the sound of the word and the way it rolls off her tongue. I say this because in most of her conversations, the word *Worcester* would take center stage. If she talked about how cold or hot the weather is, she would finish off by saying "I bet it's not that cold in Worcester" or "I'm sure it's hotter in Worcester" or "I hope the ice storm won't hit Worcester" or "I heard Worcester will get a lot of rain this spring" (and this is only in reference to the weather). There is no end—any subject, any conversation, any report is paired or compared to Worcester.

A number of times, after being in the lobby mumbling, talking, and being friendly with the doorman, she would return to her unit or apartment, then call the desk phone asking the doorman on duty, "Can you please come up to my apartment and help me open my prescription container?" or sometimes it's a jar of pickles or jam. Upon arriving at her apartment, we see clearly that she is only pretending not to be able to open the container, but despite the obvious, we would play along and help her with the task, even though there have been times when after going up to help, she would later that day or the next day accuse us of stealing her jewelry (after cleverly hiding them).

After her accusations, Beulah will return to the lobby a day or two later to talk and mumble as if nothing ever happened. Two days after one of her grand accusations, she came down looking even older than ever, wearing her bed slippers and crumpled sleeping frock or gown. Her oversized white sport socks rolled down or dropped at her ankles. She stood at the window bent over with her left hand taking turns at times holding her lower back or straightening her glasses on her face as if checking to see if it is still there. She stood gazing intensely at an old woman with a cane and a shawl walking very slowly, moving at snail's pace on the opposite side of the street. Beulah gazed and gazed at the woman, then suddenly (with her gaze still fixed on the lady) in a high-pitched tone said, "Look at that old geezer. She can barely walk. I know her. Her name is Vera. She will soon fall apart."

Whenever she is asked, questioned, or challenged about her antics or comments, she will always respond by placing her hand back side up, under her chin, and with a sometimes slow, sometimes swift forward or sweeping motion with her tongue sticking halfway out pressed between lips to make a fartlike sound in sync with the forward motion of her hand as if to say get lost, I don't give a hoot, who cares, or piss off.

With Beulah, one never knows what she is up to or what words, comments, or actions to expect. Maybe its dementia, senility, or an old brain overloaded with tricks. One cold winter night while on duty at the desk, the phone rang. It was Beulah on the other end, saying, "Help, I've fallen, and I can't get up."

For a moment, I thought that maybe I was listening to a TV commercial, but suddenly flashed back to reality and smiled, because I knew where she got the phrase. She then continued, "Can you please come up to help me up from the floor?" After hearing this, my first thought was to call 911 (the paramedics) to help her, but because I knew that she is as tricksy as Smigel, I decided to check out the situation before making the call. I got to her unit door forgetting that I did not bring the master key. My hand instinctively held and twisted the knob, and not surprisingly, the door was unlocked. Into the apartment I walked. Slowly, while shouting, "Hello, hello," I saw Beulah lying on her side with one arm outstretched toward me and saying, "Help, help!" The telephone was neatly seated on the floor next to her; at that point, I was sure that she was up to something. Because if she had fallen, how could the phone be so neatly positioned on the floor next to her?

Nevertheless, I went over to help her up. After helping her to her feet (which did not require much effort), she asked, "Can you help me to my bed?" which I did. Then she asked, "Can you please tuck me in." I pulled the blanket over her, making sure that she was well covered and warm. I said goodnight to her, and as I turned and walked toward the door to leave, I heard as if a knife sliced the air in the room, "Can you give me a goodnight kiss?"

I momentarily froze with my back toward her. I slowly spun around facing her to see her face in the dimly lit room looking pale and pitiful. I reluctantly and hesitantly walked over to her bed. In my head I said to myself, "Leave, just turn around and leave, but another voice in my head said, "There is no harm in giving her a peck on the forehead." Reluctantly, I leaned over to do just that when I felt her arms round my back and with strength I could not have imagined she had. She swiftly pulled me down toward her, her mouth all over my face, which I kept twisting from side to side to avoid mouth-to-mouth contact. Being stronger than her, I slowly pushed upward with my palms on the bed to separate myself from her, then with one hand, I gently, but firmly pulled her arms away. I then made my way out quickly without looking back. A few days after, I arrived at the building to begin my shift, I observed an EMS vehicle pulling away from the front of the building. The doorman I relieved related to me that Beulah was taken to the hospital due to a stroke. I was extremely saddened by the news because despite all of her antics, she was a lonely soul caught in an existence that can be at times cruel and unforgiving.

Then at that moment, my mind and thoughts flashback to the feelings I experienced when I got the news that my own mother had died of a stroke. She was only fifty years young. The last I heard was that Beulah later ended up in a nursing home and died shortly after.

DOUGLAS

Douglas lives in a building adjacent to this high-rise. He also lives in his own world. Our thoughts, ways, practices, and ideas are all alien to him. His world is total simplicity. He has no ambitions, no aspirations, no plans, no ideas, no ideals, and I would go as far as saying, in his mind, he has no problems.

His mind is the mind of a child. In all of his fifty-eight years on this earth, Douglas has never had a girlfriend, never had sex or even came close to having it. He has never owned or driven a car. He gets but very few pieces of mail each month (unlike the rest of us who get loads of bills and junky, crappy stuff every day or every month). In this era where privacy is a thing of the past and everyone's life or information is floating in cyberspace waiting to be randomly accessed by whoever wants it for whatever reason, Douglas has nothing to worry about in this respect. Because his whole existence is so low key that his life or bio is not anywhere to be found in the cloud.

It is truly rare in this day and age that anyone can live in this electronically organized society and remain under the radar. A society in which we are slaves to our phones, computers, credit cards, bills, mortgages, rent, auto loans, equity loans, personal loans, payday loans, insurance of all sorts, and the list goes on. All of this just to keep the colossal and ruthless machine (which is organized society) grinding along. Douglas has almost escaped this plight. He does not have a driver's license, credit card, insurance, loans of any sort, mortgage, or anything to track. He lives in a room in an apartment that he shares with someone who sublets it to him; he cannot read, write, or express himself the way others can. His words and expressions are the simplest of simple. Like Heinrich, his mode of transportation is a bicycle and, in rare occasions, the train.

One trait that Douglas shares along with the rest of us is that he has weaknesses and habits; in this case, it is eating toys and fishing. Douglas eats almost any and everything he gets his hands on. If it is edible or close to edible, he'll eat it. Like a ritual, he eats three to four bowls of cereal (Frosted Flakes) in the morning. Along with the cereal, he consumes anywhere from four to twelve eggs every morning.

With his childlike mind, he frequently stops by the desk to tell me what he ate, when, and where. Pertaining to breakfasts he will often ask, "Guess how many eggs I had this morning," and before I can make a guess, he would always answer his own question by saying eight, nine, or twelve. On the lawns, at the front and sides on this building and other buildings in this neighborhood, we observe little bunnies or rabbits. After dark, they can be seen nibbling on grass and other plants. While myself and others will gaze quietly at them in admiration and would do anything to protect them from danger or harm, knowing that they are trying to survive and also add some balance between man and nature in this urban setting or environment, Douglas, on the other hand, is constantly trying every possible way to catch, cook, and eat them. Luckily for them, he has not been successful in his efforts and with his snares. Once he almost caught one, when one night he snuck up behind it and threw a cardboard box over it. The poor little thing was so frightened and scared that it jumped, shook the box off, and bolted for its dear life.

Whenever Douglas buys the pie, one half gallon of ice cream, or a family-size bag of potato chips, he eats them all at once while watching his favorite programs, reruns of *The Honeymooners*, *Gilligan's Island*, and *Bonanza*. On several occasions while bicycling to or from work (bagging groceries in a supermarket), he would stop to pick up a dead squirrel that was recently killed by cars. He then takes them home, skins, clean, cook, and eat them. On the days when he is not at work bagging groceries, Douglas can be found at his favorite fishing spot, behind an apartment complex at a river that runs through the center of town, and it is my belief that any river that runs through the city is most likely polluted, but polluted or not, it matters not to Douglas because everything he catches, he eats.

At times when the fish are not biting, he would look around for frogs, and if he spots one, he will hit it with a rock, then take it home to meet his awaiting frying pan. It is said that everyone is blessed with a talent of some sort, whatever that talent might be. Douglas's talent is truly unique. He farts on demand.

Whenever challenged or asked to prove it, he always obliges. Whether it be ten, twenty, fifty, one hundred, he rips them out consecutively. He is truly a flatulent man. Not only does he farts on demand, he is also a compulsive farter. During any conversation with Douglas, every three to five minutes, he will utter the words "boy, excuse me" then move toward the door, open it, stick his ass outside with his head still on the inside, blow out a pent-up fart that would be so loud that it echoes back into the lobby. When told to remain outside so that it can be aired out and to not bring it back inside with him, he would stand inside at the door, holding it open with one arm while using a fanning or sweeping motion with the other trying to push the remnant of the odor out.

Douglas is the total opposite of an intellectual acrobat. He cannot hold complex conversations or thoughts. He knows next to nothing about the three Rs: reading, writing, and arithmetic. Philosophy, art, and science are alien to him. Aside from his old flip phone, the only other tech device he owns is his Sony Walkman, which uses cassette tapes on which he listens to his favorite artists: Shania Twain, Dixie Chicks, and Alan Jackson. He holds no grudges, envy, ill thoughts, or bad wishes for anyone. If everyone on this earth was like Douglas, there would be no conflicts, hatred, or prejudice. His bicycle and food are his major concerns.

THE FEARFUL

Fear—one of the most dreaded word in any language. Even the sound of the word is fearful in itself. Fear manifest itself in many forms—fear of failure, fear of success, fear of the truth, fear of the future, fear of others, fear of ghosts or the supernatural, fear of the unknown, fear of death, fear of fear, and a list goes on and on.

This high-rise has its fair share of the fearful. During the years I have spent in this humble position, I have gotten to know some individuals a bit more closely than just casually. I have quietly listened to their tales, life stories, disappointments, and tragedies. I have looked into their eyes and seen their anguish, pain, despair, and frustration, and there were times when all of these emotions are bundled together like a wounded and trapped animal.

Clyde is a man consumed by a morbid fear that someone is out to get him. Clyde lives on the sixteenth floor of this high-rise, a building with only sixteen floors, but he swears that he often hears footsteps running up the stairwell and people entering the vacant apartment above, taking showers, and moving furniture around, causing commotion and disturbance. He feels certain that these activities are done on purpose and aimed solely at him. He does not join or participate in any way in social medias, with the fear that if he participates in these activities, they will attract his imaginary predators. He refrains from shaking hands with anyone in fear of catching some form of disease. Clyde is a retired person who is mostly holed up in his apartment, but the minute he emerges from his sanctuary, he becomes even more paranoid. He glances in a 180-degree field every few steps he takes.

Perhaps Clyde's worst fear is the fear of our ever-advancing technology. The leaps and bounds of the electronic and digital world have him frightened. The very private and reclusive person that he is, he's paranoid that any or everyone will now have knowledge of his whereabouts, his every move, and everything about him. He once expressed to me that if he had the power to do so, he would erase every social media, every internet search engine, every app, and even though he admits that it has some degree of merit, he would also eliminate the entire internet.

His belief is that privacy has a place in our lives, and now that it is no more, he would like to see things return to simplicity. In his mind, utter simplicity is utter bliss.

He fails to understand why our government has given so much rein to these tech giants, and now they all but have total control of our lives and the way we think; he has resigned to the fact that there is no stopping this force, yet hopeful that what goes around will eventually come around, and the horse and buggy days will return. Like the alleged Unabomber, he swears that our pursuit of technology will eventually destroy us.

MRS. WAKEFIELD

Mrs. Wakefield is a very quiet and peaceful person. A woman of about eighty-seven years old with multiple health problems, of which half of these health issues shows their ugly faces on the outside in various forms—limping to the point where she depends on a walker or a cane, black and blue spots along with bruises acquired from the many falls she had, hands that at times shakes uncontrollably, lips that tremble when she speaks and sometimes even when not speaking.

The other half are the issues inside such as heart problems, high blood pressure, diabetes, and a host of other ailments. Her daughter and grandchildren who visit her quite often are equally as sweet as she is. Unlike the scores of others in similar physical state in this high-rise, she never complained about any of her ailments or the degree or extent of her immobility. Even as she tries with all of her might to fight back, both emotionally and physically to win over these maladies and to recapture her vibrant youthful years, yet in a strange juxtaposition or paradox, seemingly unexplainable, she, like a silent and deep river or a calm yet strong fortress, will at times quietly accept her inevitable decline.

Often times after a visit from her daughter and grandchildren, or re-entering the building from one of her short but determined walks, I would greet her in a friendly, compassionate, and encouraging way. She would sometimes express or show a brief smile along with tears quietly rolling down her face. In those moments, I tried to read her emotions, her face, the teardrops rolling down her face, and in those same moments, I could see myself, my mother, my sister, my brother, my friends, my enemies, all of us. I could see the humanity in her eyes, and the brotherhood that I felt in those moments was a feeling of the connection of one human being to another.

In her eyes, I could see fear, a fear that I could not determine, the fear of death or maybe fear of the unknown, fear of dying and leaving her daughter and grandchildren behind. A fear of pain, a fear of nothingness, or maybe all of these fears combined.

In those moments also, I reflect on the state of our existence as human beings (although some of us are not worthy of this title; critters may be more appropriate). Our greed, our wants, our hatred of others who may not look or share the same values, our cruelty, our destructive ways, our propensity for conflicts, and even though we are strong in many ways in our creativity, our ability to erect skyscrapers and bridges, to build supercomputers, microchips and processors, to recover from natural disasters, to build super-speed machines, etc.

Yet we are weak, to acknowledge that we are one human family, one race—the human race—weak to respect and accept each other. Weak to accept and learn from other cultures, weak to see that we and all life forms are somehow connected, and weak to see that in order to survive, we must learn how to live in peace and harmony with one another.

I saw in Mrs. Wakefield's eyes a suffering deep within, and behind this suffering, I also saw hope. I saw hope through the love she had for her children and through her pain and suffering. Instead of anger, she quietly and calmly displayed kindness and respect to all around her.

Mrs. Wakefield died with tears in her eyes and I cannot help wondering if in her mind those tears were for hope for us or tears of sorrow for us.

OSWALD
AKA EL HOMBRE
BORACHO

Oswald is always drunk at any given time of any given day; any place anywhere the stench of today's, yesterday's and maybe week's old alcohol combined is his cologne. When speaking with him in person, it is advisable to keep a safe distance (about two steps back from the normal personal space comfort zone). If this precaution is not taken, one would be hit with what can be called a tidal wave of alcohol stink and odor so penetrating that, if standing too close, you will feel and taste it in your throat and your nose will burn.

The amazing thing about Oswald and others like him is they don't seem to smell the stink they tote around. They seem to be completely oblivious to it. I say this because he has a woman who he refers to as his sweetie pie. Though not as bad as him, she also smells and both their alcohol odors are to them completely acceptable.

And oh, what an interesting couple they make. He's a short but wiry figure who would be liken to a guy called Shrimpy. She's tall and massive, with huge tits and ass. Of course for Oswald, these attributes could be even bigger. "The bigger, the better," he often expressed.

Yet even though he is the smaller of the duo, he tries to rule with fists of iron, and at times when she stands her ground, there will be fights so loud that the phone at the desk starts ringing like crazy, with neighbors complaining "they are at it again," and on many occasions, the police had to intervene.

It is said that all short men possess a distinct complex. They are so self-conscious about their lack of height that they try to make up for it by empowering themselves in whatever way they can or however they can. In Oswald's case, he tries his hardest with his personality and behavior to tower over his woman like a colossal. He is also fond of guns, of which he has quite a few in his collection. He often boasts about his guns and people he would like to take out. Aside from being short, Oswald, however, has another complex, one that is entrenched deep within. He has a dreadful fear that foreigners are taking over the country (which is ironic, because he is also a foreigner).

He particularly vents a great percentage of his rage and ranting against people from Latin America. According to him, they are everywhere he goes; they even took over his favorite fishing spot, to the extent that it is impossible for him to get a place to stand in order to cast his line, and to make matters worse, he swears that from his observations, those guys don't throw anything back. The fish can be as small as a minnow or as big as Moby Dick, they take it home. When Oswald is fishing, it is a sight to behold. Each cast produces a movement like a ballet dancer, and when the cast is complete, he assumes a Shakespearian stance, and it is for these sweeping, poetic movements that he needs his fishing area clear.

Oswald watches and scrutinizes every person who moves into the building. He even scrutinizes visitors, and only a few are good enough. Only a few measures up to his criteria and expectations. If you are a male member of the majority in society and have admiration for and show support for a certain political party and a certain candidate of that party who utters derogatory remarks about immigrants and women, then you will have his approval. If you happen to be a black woman, you will also get his approval.

He has an obsession with and an attraction to black women, and the bigger they are, the greater the attraction. I've heard others refer to his woman as Mount Everbreast, for the simple reason that she is overly endowed in that part of her anatomy.

Another one of my observations about Oswald is that when he speaks about women (and when in his case means all his waking hours), he speaks only of their physical attributes and their genitals or private parts; he thinks, dreams, and talks about pussy, constantly. On one occasion during one of his pussy lectures, he leaned over the desk (so far over that I thought he would tumble over and smother me) and uttered, "If you stop thinking about pussy, you are dead." Not once have I ever heard him talking about the smarts, talents, values, and contributions of women in society.

Often times, I've had to stop him in his tracks to remind him that women are much smarter than us men and that he should listen to Harry Belafonte's song with the lyrics "that's right the woman is smarter, smarter than a man in every way," but these words mean nothing to him because of his short man's complex and his addiction to the bottle, which combined gives us an angry, frustrated, little man who appeases himself by proclaiming himself king in his own feeble little mind.

A little man who wants to get rid of and shows himself above Hispanics, Indians, black men, and most women.

Some years ago, I was up very late, flipping through channels on the television. I finally ended up watching a comedian expressing his thoughts on politics and politicians. He was very at ease and smooth as he delivered his expressions. He said something that I will always remember. He said, "The capitalists mentality is, when a man is down, don't hit him, kick him, it is easier.'" Oswald has adopted this mentality and lives by it.

JERRY, STANLEY, RICH, AND OTHERS

These are guys who are residents in this high-rise, guys who are all bachelors, who range in ages from twenties to fifties. Some are owners and some are renters. They are all ladies' men or womanizers who just can't seem to get enough of women.

These guys would not have to live in such tension and fear if they had just one, two, or three ladies. Each of these guys have multiple partners who comes and goes at various times of the day and night.

Try as they may, they cannot get a grip on the inevitable clashes and confrontations, so they depend on us the doormen to at times stall, distract or lie for them and to the women.

There were times when even though all precautions were taken, mishaps and unpleasant confrontations took place. The interesting thing here is these women, each and every one of them, are of the belief that they are the only one. I once made an error when Rich called the desk and said, "If lady B shows up, don't let her up. Send her away." My mistake was that I thought he had said the opposite, and I sent her up not knowing that he had another lady up there.

This lady whom he had up there had arrived prior to my shift and was helping him with his laundry, and because the laundry machines are situated outside the units in the common hallways, lady A was walking back from the laundry room to the unit where the door was left ajar, and at that same time lady B got off the elevator and also walked toward the unit door, so they both went in together, and the shit hit the fan.

I learned that Rich hinted that lady A was his cleaning lady and that was when all hell broke loose. Needless to say, Rich at that moment felt as if he just wanted to melt and become one with the floor, and of course, the blame was on me.

I thoroughly messed up. It ended up that Rich lost both ladies but did not come down too hard on me. In just a few days, he was back to his old tricks, and I learned the hard way to never allow this ever to happen again.

Stanley is a renter with a roommate who is just as promiscuous as he is. They share a spacious two-bedroom unit on one of the higher floors, and they are party animals.

They like to throw parties. During those wild parties, calls came in to the desk in rapid succession from neighbors complaining about the noise and rowdiness, and that people were on the balcony throwing beer bottles off and onto the grounds below.

It's miraculous that none of those bottles ever hit anyone. These parties would go on into the later part of the night where I would have to go up to ask them to keep the noise level down. On some of these occasions, when Stanley or his roommate would come to open the door (usually after several minutes of banging on the door), he would have a woman hanging on to him, clad only in her little itsy-bitsy giggling while saying, "Come back, Stan."

What is also interesting is Stan and his roommate each have a woman who are often presented or introduced as their one and only main squeezes, but these main squeezes are never to be seen at the parties because they were never invited. Neither of them have any knowledge of these parties, because they were never told, and this is where Stan and his roommate's fears set in, because even though the ladies are told well in advance of the parties by their men that they (Stan and Jerry) will be out of town on business on that particular day, these cheaters have this fear that their women might just show up at any time during the parties for whatever reason.

Prior to and during these events, Stan and Jerry would be our (the doorman's) best friends. They will stop at the desk and slip a fifty dollar bill to the man on duty, then mumble in a low tone, "If my lady shows up, please say that we are away or out of town for a few days and you are not allowed to give access to anyone without a written authorization, then make sure that they leave." Luckily for us, we never had to lie for them regarding these parties because the ladies obviously believed the lies they were being told. So far, they haven't shown up while any of these parties are thrown.

It's either these guys have gotten so used to what they do, or they are completely heartless because two days after the wild party, they would pass through the lobby with their main squeezes on their arms, like nothing happened. Totally the opposite of the anxiety and fear displayed shortly before and during these wild parties.

One might ask, "If these guys and others like them have their main squeezes or significant others, wives, etc., then why the need for these parties, of which most of the revelers also have their own wives, husbands, or significant others?" I and the other doormen have our own theory. We believe that these party animals are in need of and are seeking something other than the norm. Their lives are perhaps boring, mundane, lackluster socially, personally, sexually, and more.

These wild parties and the activities and reveling that goes on there give them release, relief, and a sense of freedom—freedom from a dull existence, a robotlike existence where they get up in the mornings, eat the same breakfast, probably some of the following: bacon and eggs, toast, coffee, etc. They tumble off to work, after kissing their wives or partners goodbye for the day, then they sit either in their cars, in traffic, or the train, or the bus with the other robots, all gazing into space while wondering "is this it, is there more to life than this routine, this seemingly endless cycle, like stairs that leads to nowhere or dropping a rock into a dark well and listening, listening for the plunk that is not coming, then getting to the job and having to deal with the offices bitches, assholes, and jerks, also called coworkers. The good, sincere, and considerate are few and hard to find; and when the day is over, they tumble home and prepare to start the cycle all over again. This repetitive, monotonous cycle appears to be more of a burden than a lifestyle.

They tell me that there are no such things as
monsters and vampires and saints and angels …
But I found them all in my neighbors.

—Kahlil Gibran

GIRVAN WILCOX
(AKA MR. CLEAN)

Mr. Clean is a longtime resident of this high-rise. He is a forerunner, been here since dirt, as one of the few who were the first to move into the building when it was all rentals, and when it was converted to condos, they bought their units at bargain prices. Mr. Clean is one of the handful of surviving forerunners. The others have either died, went to nursing homes, assisted living, or moved to Florida or to warmer climate.

Mr. Clean got his nickname from two folds. One is he has a stark resemblance to the animated figure used to advertise a certain cleaning agent. Number two is that he smells. He reeks of garlic at all times, so the term Mr. Clean is used paradoxically. Tall, overweight, bald head, and sweaty are a few of the words that describes Girvan, a.k.a. Mr. Clean.

Aside from being big, smelly, and sweaty he is also compulsively flatulent, a hater of people, and an extreme right neo-Nazi who hides it under a cloak of Catholicism and the guise of Christianity. The rosary that he carries around daily is a permanent fixture. Whenever he rides the elevators, his odor lingers for hours inside. Oftentimes even after Girvan has long exited the elevator, someone will say "Phew! What's that smell?" And another would respond, "He was here. It's him! It's Mr. Wilcox."

Unlike Oswald who hates Latinos, Mr. Wilcox hates everyone who is not American and not look like him. He has a bare face habit of just simply walking up to someone or a fellow resident, neighbor (whether it be a man or woman, and who happens to be from another country) and say, not jokingly but in a serious tone, "Go back to your country where you came from, you ugly son of a bitch."

In a local supermarket he was heard in a conversation with a cashier at the checkout point, asking her, "Where are you from?"

A certain country in Asia, she replied.

"And what is the weather or climate like there?"

"Warm and comfortable," was her response.

"And the people?"

"Friendly and beautiful," she answered.

At that point, Girvan belted out, "Then why are you here? You should go be back to your paradise!"

The astonished girl was so taken aback that she was at a loss for words.

This was not a random incident. Girvan has done this to many unsuspecting foreigners who at first thought he was a charming person who was just simply showing some interest in them and their countries. Then to their surprise, the monster came out.

Whatever degree of a softer side he has (and believe me, it's not much) comes out when he sees young or teenage American girls preferably white. He tries to get friendly with them, striking up conversations in a tone of voice that borders on coming onto. On another occasion, he was seen at a local beach chatting up a group of girls who were heard responding to him, saying, "Get away from us, you creep."

Like Dexter, Girvan drives a huge old Lincoln town car, and due to lack of past needed maintenance, it is always in and out of a local gas station repair shop located at one corner of the intersection just a mere three-minute walk at the end of the street where this high-rise is located.

Girvan has a love-hate relationship with the owner of the gas station and his repair facility. His car has been brought there for all emergency repairs as he has done over the years when the father of the present owner was alive and ran the business.

He firmly believes that the father ran a better operation and took better care of his old jalopy than the son, but due to his loyalty to the father, he continues to use this facility. So on an almost-weekly frequency, the car is in this repair shop, and each time he walks to or from the repair facility, he of course stops in the lobby to vent his anger and displeasure about the facility, the owner, his neighbors, the neighborhood, the city, the state, the president, the government. His deceased parents whom he believed hated him for whatever reason and how if they were still alive, he would stab them over and over again, while making actual upward and downward stabbing motions using his pen to simulate a knife or dagger. His wife is not spared of his displeasure also.

I remember on one of his always-unwelcome visits to the front desk, he uttered my name, then said, "I must tell you that I made the biggest mistake of my life twenty-nine years ago." He was referring to his marriage.

Two things about Girvan that goes hand in hand with his existence. One is that he permanently reeks of garlic, and two, he is extremely flatulent. Always, while standing at the front desk, venting his anger at everyone and the world, pretending to be diplomatic and classy in his expressions, farts would be forcefully released every ten minutes, and because his farts are so dynamic and thunderous, whenever he releases one while engrossed in his discourse, at the moment of release, he would raise his voice in a loud tone in an effort to drown out the loudness and echo of the fart, and after it is released, his voice would be smoothly lowered to its usual tone.

Girvan or Mr. Wilcox is one of those individuals who has illusions of grandeur; he feels an act as if he is of the upper echelon, upper-upper, the cream of the crop, the top step on the social ladder, like Heimlich. I get the feeling that he sees all others who don't look, act, and think the same as him, that they are below him. In his mind, these are sub-humans. If not biologically, then at least in the social sense. Yet his attire, his old jalopy, the old briefcase he carries around does not support his inner thoughts and actions.

It is hard and strange to think or imagine that someone who professes Christianity, whose rosary is a permanent fixture in his hand or pocket, and a bible in his bag can harbor such dislike and unacceptability of others whom his own creator created.

I will not forget the time when Girvan, on one of his rantings, leaned over the desk with the stench of garlic coupled with his favorite drink. Southern Comfort emanating from his mouth, his clothing, and his pores, he said to me, "How many of them do you think are in the building?"

"What are you talking about?" I responded. "And who are you referring to?"

"Jews," he said. "How many do you think lives in the building?"

"Sorry, Mr. Wilcox, I do not entertain this type of talk," I said. "We are all one human family. The people you are referring to are our brothers and sisters."

Being a person of dark complexion, I immediately began to think of what he might have said to another doorman who happens to be Caucasian. I can picture him leaning over the desk and asking the other guy, "How many of them do you think are living in the building? Blacks I mean."

I cannot say for certain how the other guy would respond, but knowing him, I would guess that his response would not be the same as mine. It would be, more likely than not, in favor of Wilcox and his warped mentality, because that other doorman is a hypocrite of colossal magnitude. He speaks in favor of and agrees with whomever is next to or standing in front of him at that moment. He is incapable of expressing his own thoughts or feelings on any controversial matter. This other guy and Mr. Wilcox are bosom buddies because he agrees with and tells him what he wants to hear.

During all these years in which Girvan Wilcox have been going about insulting and degrading many individuals and classes of people, I was pleased to see the occasion when one woman stood up to him, stood up for her rights, and challenged him.

In this high-rise, like many others, there is a common room called a lounge where residents are allowed to use for get-togethers, parties, or meetings. Girvan's unit is across the hallway from this room, and whenever a party is held by one of his neighbors or fellow residents, he will go, without being invited, mingling, chatting, socializing, and partaking of their food and drinks, then just as quietly as he appeared at the gathering, he would quietly disappear and about thirty minutes to an hour later, he would reappear, not in a quiet way, but clapping and stomping his fist on a table while shouting, "Time to go, break it up, lickety-split, too much noise. My wife and I need to rest, and you are disturbing us. Stop the party now and get out." On this particular evening, Marla was having a birthday party for her niece. Girvan showed up and did the same thing. She knew of his past behavior pattern and encounters with others so she was somewhat prepared to take him on.

She walked over to him and said, "No, we will not leave. We are allowed to use this room for 'X' amount of hours and we are only half of that time into our party, so therefore, you leave now."

"I most certainly will not," he replied.

Then another person in the room shouted, "But you were here only a short while ago, partying with us and having a good time."

Upon hearing that, he again shouted, "Get out!"

Marla then moved closer to him, saying, "Mr. Wilcox, how can a person like yourself who claims to have a PhD in adult education behave in the manner in which you do? Leave *now*, Mr. Wilcox!"

He then turned red with rage, and in a matter of seconds, they were in each other's face with the tips their noses almost touching with him saying, "I'm a doctor. You will refer to me as Dr. Wilcox."

And Marla blared back "Mr. Wilcox." And the blaring went back and forth, with nose tips sometimes touching, and saliva wetting each other's face, like Daffy Duck spitting in the face of Bugs Bunny in their shouting match "rabbit season or duck season." In their case, it went "Mr. Wilcox" "Dr. Wilcox" "Mr. Wilcox" "Dr. Wilcox" "Mr. Wilcox" "Dr. Wilcox." I guess, the rage that ensued was so heated that she totally ignored the garlic-lased odor coming at her in full strength and force.

Needless to say, the tension was so high that the police was called to intervene and to separate the two. To my knowledge, since that incident, he never again bothered her, because whenever and wherever she sees him, she stares him down as if to say, "You want to try something again?"

Even though he didn't bother with Marla anymore, he kept on doing the same to others. I guess if one stands his or her ground and not back away from a bully, then the bully loses.

Thinking about Girvan, his selfish outlook on life, his twisted ways, his heartless behavior, it makes one wonder and ask, how can a person who espouses Christianity, claims to be deeply religious, carries a rosary around with him at all times, says he believes in the bible, and purports that Jesus Christ is his savior harbors so much hatred, misguided thoughts, ill wishes, and dislike for his fellow human brothers and sisters, simply because of their social and/or economic status and the brownness of their skin? I guess he didn't do his research to enlighten himself of the fact that his savior, Jesus, was born to a mother and father who were not high on the social ladder, were, by all means, not rich, and more likely than not, they were of brown complexion, because of the climate and the characteristic of people from that region; also, someone ought to remind Mr. Wilcox that his Lord and Savior was not American and was also Jewish.

With Girvan, like most us, change does not come easily, or mostly not at all, even when we are aware that what we are doing is not right and is harmful to ourselves and to others.

Therefore, change of any kind often requires courage, and courage requires change, so both are intertwined in a marital state that cannot be separated and that we all need to adopt.

One may say that for Girvan to make any kind of change in his outlook and behavior is hopeless due to his advanced age along with decades of his ingrained feeling of the false sense of superiority over women, foreigners, and others. I think he tells himself, "Here I am, strong and mighty, a first-world white man. In America, the greatest first-world country ever known, all those who aspire to come to my land of plenty, get behind me or fall to your knees in my presence."

It is said that "One can never teach an old dog new tricks or that it is impossible to change the mind-set of an older person. I strongly disagree with those statements. I believe anyone can change if they do just as the singer Bob Marley said, "Open your eyes and look within."

The only thing that prohibits a person from making that change is death, and in Girvan's case, death came before change. The strong and mighty Girvan Wilcox became ill with multiple complaints—high blood pressure, heart disease, arthritis, bladder problems, etc. He deteriorated slowly, unable to hold his bodily wastes.

He would fall very often, a few times a day. The few times when I was called to come up to help in getting him up from his chair, I had to hold my breath in an effort to avoid the overwhelming stench of urine and feces that he left in his pants.

A few months before he died, an aide was hired to help with taking care of him. At that point, he had no strength to tell his aide (a humble woman from Haiti) to go back to where she came from.

MRS. WILCOX, GIRVAN'S WIFE

Even though he thought (in his words) that he made the biggest mistake of his life when he married her, in many ways, I believe, Libby and Girvan were meant for each other, standing back and observing them together. The way in which they moved around, spoke, and engaged each other, lost in a world of their own, using words, tones, and mannerisms of the so-called upper class to complement each other.

Libby Gertrude Wilcox displayed all the characteristics of the rich and famous, her attire, her choices of words (even though old-fashioned), the topics she opened up for discussions at social gatherings. At tea time, she sips with lips pouting and pinky sticking out while daintily holding the cup. To observe her at these gatherings, you would get the feeling that she thinks she is a duchess, yet with all this display of finesse, she is a hopeless alcoholic who can easily guzzle a full bottle of scotch daily. Her husband Girvan is just about the same as she is, both drunkards. And when they got drunk, they fought like cats and dogs.

I was told that this had been going on for many years, but on the flip side of their togetherness, when they are not drunk and are together in public or wherever, they would put on a show worthy of being called Romeo and Juliet or the great pretenders. They are like two lovebirds doting over each other as if they either are the perfect couple, or doing a damn good job of pretending to be. On the other hand, I was also told (and have seen firsthand) that in the past, the cops had to be called to intervene often when their arguments and fights got physical.

When one tries to figure out why they fight so much just as often as they play lovebirds, it's like a fifty-fifty love-hate deal. Maybe it's because politically, he is extreme right, where she, on the other hand, is extreme left, but not nearly as extreme as he is, and knowing him any opposition to his ideologies means war (quite similar to a certain political candidate who campaigned for the presidency of the United States of America).

Or it could be that they are members of two different religious beliefs. He is a staunch Catholic and she is Episcopalian, and because she doesn't drive, on Sundays, he has the duty of dropping her off at her church before continuing on to his, and when both services are over, he picks her up again homeward bound. Only a fly on the headliner of that car would be able to divulge what is politically and/ or religiously discussed during these car rides, and as we all know quite well, these are extremely sensitive subjects, even when engaged in with the people closest to us, more so when one or both party are blinded fanatics.

It made matters worse when after a night of heavy indulgence with their favorite liquors, they leave for church still under the influence of contenders like Johnny Walker, Jim Beam, Southern Comfort, Jack Daniels, etc., all aboard the SS *Cutty Sark*.

I can recall the time, on a hot summer night, when both Girvan and Libby were at it again, drinking heavily, getting into sporadic arguments, and bickering.

The phone rang at the front desk. There was a resident and neighbor of the Wilcox's on the other end reporting that they had heard loud arguments and noises coming from the Wilcox's apartment and that it eventually spilled over into the hallway. I went up to see what was really going on, and of course, there was Mrs. Wilcox in the hallway in a drunken state, walking in an unsteady manner. I was about twenty-five to thirty feet away from her, then as soon as she saw me, she began walking toward me with her right arm held out and upward, as if trying to catch something falling from above while uttering words that were unclear, and in my mind, I couldn't help but wonder, "What the hell is she saying and what is she trying to catch?"

She kept on moving directly toward me reaching upward, and her words that were becoming clearer as she got closer also got louder. She still kept on coming toward me as if she didn't care that we were about to have a head-on collision. At the last few seconds, I quickly shifted to one side to avoid the collision.

I heard her saying, as she held her arm out and upward like catching at soapy bubbles blown from a child's wand. "I'm brilliant, I'm brilliant, I'm brilliant," and as she kept on repeating those words, with a glazed look in her eyes and smiling as if being appeased by her own declaration about herself, she then turned around and was again heading toward me. To avoid a repeat of all that mishigas I made it quickly to the elevator and hopped in just in time to avoid her brilliance.

I returned to the lobby and got settled in again, answering phone calls and logging all the complaints coming in. Until you undertake a job like this or similar jobs, you would never imagine the various complaints people have or encounter just by trying to live the life of modern humans, or to put it another way "by just playing the survival game in our modern society."

It didn't take long for the call from the Wilcox's unit to come in. It was Mr. Wilcox on the phone asking me to please run up to assist him in lifting Libby from the floor. Just after declaring her brilliance, she fell hard, due to liquor consumption and who knows what else.

I wouldn't put anything beyond her husband's capability, because a sail on the *SS Cutty Sark* can shift even the strongest minds among us temporarily into neutral then into realms unknown.

One Sunday morning, he dropped her off at the front door, which I thought was unusual, because they have a reserved indoor parking space where they always park after church then go up to their unit, but on this particular morning, after dropping her off, he sped away like a jack rabbit, and she entered the lobby fuming to such a degree that she literally turned red. I watched and waited to see if smoke would be ejected from her ears. Then she began to spill all the details as they all do at the lobby desk. She explained that they just had the most heated argument that almost resulted in a fistfight. She continued, fuming, that Girvan had gone to church in a drunken state, and during the mass, he interrupted the priest and challenged him, asking him why he had women on the altar and told the priest in no uncertain term that women are not to be on or anywhere around the altar, and that it is written in the Bible, so the word should obeyed and who does the priest think he is to be breaking the law or the Word of the Lord.

Libby was angry because she saw her husband's stance as an attack on women, no respect for the opposite sex, and a blatant disregard for equality and the rights of women; she is very aware of his hatred of the feminist movement and that he thinks the noted feminist Gloria Steinem is nothing but a bitch, but this time, she said, "He had gone too far." In her words, "He had shot his load." She had had enough and will not entertain his crap any longer. "To hell with him," she said.

In another blowout or incident, which took place on a cool October night, there I was, sitting at the desk or round table with the doors propped open, enjoying a delicious breeze flowing through the lobby, when suddenly, a noise echoed through the lobby and sliced the quiet calmness of the moment, like the swiftness of a guillotine. I looked quickly to my right, and there was Libby, tightly gripping onto the handrail at the stairs, trying to keep her balance so that she would not topple over from being overly intoxicated.

She paused midway down the short stairs, wobbling, while gripping on even more tightly than the previous minute, reeking from the smell of scotch or whiskey. She continued down the steps while saying, "I have called the cops to arrest Girvan and to take him away." I could not resist in asking why and for what reason.

She replied, "Don't ask me why, and in fact, don't ask me anything at all. I have called the police. They are on their way here and that's that."

She made it to a chair and her entire body just dropped on it. Luckily. it had armrest. If it didn't, she would have toppled off in one continuous motion.

As she sat mumbling incoherently, two officers arrived. I greeted and informed them that she is the one who called. They went over toward her. She was so out of it that for a moment she didn't realize that they had arrived, but as soon as she did, she started talking non-stop. The officers who could barely get a word in asked, "Lady, where is your husband?"

She responded, "Upstairs in the apartment." He told her they would talk to her in the lobby, then they would go up and talk to him separately while she remained in the lobby.

She continued telling the officers that Girvan punched her, then pushed her backward into the bathtub, and threatened to stab her, because she did not refer to him as Dr. Wilcox, "And he's no doctor," she exclaimed. "Years ago, he took a correspondence course through the mail, which he did not even complete. Since then he swears and lies about having a PhD." She went on telling the officers that "several years ago, he did the same thing, punched me, pushed me into the tub, and tried to stab me, for the same reason, and since then we haven't had intercourse."

Upon hearing that, one officer looked up and rolled his eyes while the other struggled to hold back a chuckle.

At this point, the officers told her to stay put while they go up to question Mr. Wilcox, which of course she did not obey. As soon as they boarded one elevator, she stumbled into the other and up she went.

I don't know what transpired up there, but after about forty-five minutes, the officers came down and, before leaving, asked me how often are they this drunk. They then left without arresting anyone. Ten minutes after, Girvan came down, asking, "What did that bitch tell the police? Please tell me, what did she say?"

I said to him, "I don't think you would want to know, Mr. Wilcox." After pleading and insisting that I tell him what she told them, I finally gave in and told him.

Obviously, he denied all of her accusations and labeled her a wacky drunken lying schizophrenic. "And furthermore," he continued, "the part about not having intercourse for several years, yes, she is right, I have not with her, but I've had it with others."

At that moment I pictured Mr. Wilcox walking around with his rosary beads trying to project his piety and obedience to the Lord's laws and commands, yes, this is Girvan who confronted the priest and challenged him to obey God's words and commands, yet it is quite clear that he lies, gets intoxicated, and fornicates. The hypocrisy of his words and actions is astounding. If you ask me, I would say that he missed his calling. He should have been a politician.

Believe it or not, after all of these happenings, those two still lived together in the same apartment and continued to portray and pretend to those who did not know them very well that they are the perfect couple. Then I began to wonder how many among us, what percentage of the loving couples we see around us (our neighbor, friends, associates, doctors, teachers, pastors, counselors, and the list goes on) are just putting on a show, pretending to be happy together, pretending to be the model couple, when deep down and behind closed doors, they are not happy, not satisfied. They are like oil and water, but some of us try to endure and suffer through it for the sake of a child, children or for financial reasons while others pretend for the sake of societal and social expectations, norms, and stigma, but the reality is and will continue till the end of time. Some among us fall in love, then at some point, fall out of love.

DOGFACE

Ralphie, a.k.a. Dogface, is a fellow doorman in this high-rise. According to people who have known him for many years, he earned the name Dogface because, when he gets up in the mornings from his slumber, his eyes and jaws droops, like that of a bull mastiff.

Dogface epitomizes the phrase "with a friend like that, who needs enemies." He is someone like "Mack the Knife," a scoundrel, a backstabber, a reprobate, a wretch, yet he puts on a great show. He is the touchy-feely type (or so he pretends), who would be patting your back, hugging you, or holding your hand while telling you how much he loves you or how great a person you are, then the minute you walk away and out of sight, he will rip you to pieces by saying the worst things he can conjure up or fabricate about you in his little mind to anyone with a listening ear.

He is the type of person who will throw you under the bus or tractor trailer in a heartbeat. His unscrupulous ways runs deep. No one is spared the wrath of his quiet storm, and he shows no empathy for anyone or any life form. When driving, a squirrel, skunk, raccoon, etc., crossing the road in front of his car stands little chance of surviving. They would have to scramble hard and fast to get away, because he will try his hardest to run them over or scare them into the path of an oncoming vehicle, and if his goal is successful, he would glance into his rearview mirror and say something like "got you, you little fucker" then burst into a big laughing fit, which will usually last a few minutes.

Here is a scenario of the depth of Dogface's unscrupulous ways. Imagine yourself in a conversation with him, and during the conversation (while putting on his nice act), he tells you things you like to hear, praising you, saying how much he loves or likes you. With your hands being in your pocket for a while and when pulling your hand from your pocket, you accidentally pull out and drop a one hundred dollar bill, which you were not aware of, but Ralphie saw the whole thing. You would think that he would point and say, "Hey, you dropped something." No, he would rather put his size thirteen shoe to work, by stepping on it, then try to quickly end the conversation so that you can leave fast, and the second you walk away, he picks it up and pocket it.

He will do this to anyone—his so-called best friends, brother, sister, parents, cousin, grandparents, uncle, aunt, and if he had children, I'm positive he would do it to them too.

To expect Dogface changing or abandoning his ways at his point, at sixty-seven years old, is not easy at this age. He is a spoilt brat.

Throughout his life, he has never left home. He is still living at the house he grew up in with his parents who are now deceased.

He has no experience or knowledge about having to pay rent or mortgage. His parents passed away about two and a half years apart. His father was the last to go, and at that time, Dogface was already near age sixty-five.

Although change at this point for him is not impossible, it is highly unlikely. Even though he has lived at home all of his life, and even under the guidance and strictness of his parents, Dogface took to the streets, and not the good end. He hung out at the mean end with some of the most crooked, lying, thieving fiends that you can ever imagine.

The lack of empathy and scruples acquired from the mean streets is entrenched and has become a shameful part of his very existence. The only things that matters to him are expensive material stuff and money.

After numerous encounters with the law and many episodes of over indulgence in all kinds of heavy shit, which took the lives of most of his street friends, he somehow partially gave up the street life when a friend of his father pulled some strings to get him the job as a doorman.

So here we have dogface, a coworker or doorman in this high-rise, a smooth operator who mastered the art of bullshit, a doorman who tells the residents of the building whatever they want to hear and agrees and supports the religious, political, racial arguments, beliefs, and points or views of whomever is standing in front of him at that given time. He learned this technique quickly and honed it to perfection, all for the sake of getting tips and, hopefully, a big Christmas gift at the end of the year.

Ralphie has a taste for expensive things. You won't find him buying clothes at Wall Mart or any bargain store. His apparel and footwear has to be from Brooks Brothers, Saks, or other upscale stores. He has a number of Omegas, Rolexes, and other pricey watches. Salvatore Ferragamo, Polo, Maui Jim, North Face, etc., are his brands of choice, along with his sporty Mercedes Benz. He is regarded as the richest doorman around town. He is able to afford this stuff for the simple fact of never having the expenses of rent, mortgage, food, or utility bills. One resident refers to him as Ralphie Bling. A big reason for his expensive taste is he is a man trying to impress women. Unfortunately for him, and fortunately for the women, none has taken the bait.

Women somehow seem to sense in him that he is as tricksy as Smigel the Gollum. The few who took the step to give him a chance realized that not only is he trying to trick them out of whatever money they have, but he is also a kinky, nasty, perverted individual; for those reasons, he has never been able to have a girlfriend. The only physical contact he's had in the past are the ladies of the night, and I say "the past" because even those ladies found him to be too weirdly perverted, and even though they were being offered money, they wouldn't go with him a second time. He once told me that in his younger days, he turned down one woman who has willing to go to bed with him, because she wasn't hairy enough.

A couple had moved into the building where the wife, who drank a lot, gave subtle hints of being sexually dissatisfied with her husband and that he was a workaholic and never had any time for her. Dogface quickly picked up on the hints and discovered that she was wildly kinky. He made his move, and within days, they were already carrying on. Even when he was on duty, she could be seen sitting atop the desk while highly under the influence of alcohol, sometimes playing around with one foot or both feet on his shoulders, wearing a short skirt with no underwear on. It got to the point where, as soon as her husband leaves, Dogface would go up to see her, whether or not he was on duty at the desk.

Dogface is, among many other things, a tell-all, and the things he divulged to me that they both indulged in would make even Larry Flynn or Heff blush. They performed acts that go beyond the realm of sexual kinkiness, acts that the law of nature forbids, and acts that are plain and downright sick.

These encounters became a daily thing, which got weirder each time. The consumption of alcohol became an integral part, the main ingredient, the igniter of their freaky carnal acts.

One fateful evening, while heavily intoxicated, they failed in keeping their eyes on the clock, as they always did, so as to time the arrival of her husband.

So there they were, fully engaged in one of their lewd and licentious acts. Sources described the act they were engaged in as she squatting, hovering above Dogface as he lay on his back with his head under her butt, with his mouth opened wide as she filled it with pee while at the same time his right hand was busy elsewhere.

Right in the middle of their act, her husband entered the room in a classic "caught in the act" moment. I heard that he screamed like a crazy man being tortured, and that he pushed her over and away and went for Dogface. I heard that he was grabbing for anything he could get his hands on to hit Dogface with. The blow that drew some blood from Ralphie's forehead came from a clothes iron.

There was so much commotion that the neighbors from the apartments below, above, adjacent, and across the hall all called the police. While all of this was happening, the enraged husband did not even notice his wife behind him hitting him on his back with her bare hands while screaming, **"STOP IT, STOP IT, STOP IT!"**

Ralphie was arrested and taken out of the building in handcuffs; I was told that he walked through the lobby with his head hung low in embarrassment with blood on his face. The doorman on duty that night made the comment that with his head hanging, jaws drooping, and in a drunken state, he could see why Ralphie is called Dogface. His face truly looked like a mastiff.

Less than a week after this episode took place, the couple moved out of the building. They left so quietly that the neighbors had no idea that they had moved. It was as if they had just simply vanished like a puff of wind.

I figured, with the licentious activities that took place in that unit and the huge outburst that evening, they were perhaps afraid to be questioned by their nosy neighbors. And in this high-rise, like other buildings (I would imagine), gossip and news travel fast.

It is ironic that the chief spreader of gossip in the building, the bullhorn, the whistle, the trumpet, the mouth Dogface was the one who got caught in that mess.

Unlike the couple who, in shame, left quietly, Ralphie returned to work the following week, despite the many residents who voiced their objections to him being at the front desk. Many also suggested that he should be fired. But the superintendent of the building, along with a few other residents who felt sorry for him, begged the board to give him another chance, and it was reluctantly granted.

All that transpired had little effect on Dogface. He is of the streets, and the streets have given him armor against fear, shame, and sympathy. He returned like nothing ever happened and was back to his old ways—tricksy, greedy, materialistic, and zero empathy for others.

This high-rise is home to some older residents—some who are in their eighties and nineties. So from time to time, we would have ambulance out front when one falls, gets ill, or dies. Whenever Dogface is on duty and the ambulance pulls up in front, he will make comments like "Here we go again, another old fart bites the dust," or if the person is a Christian, "Now you can go to Jesus" or "It's about time." He has no second thought about making these comments regarding even those who supported the petition for him to remain employed in this high-rise.

There is so much more about Dogface that I could go on and on writing about. This lascivious person is a character, the likes of which you do not wish to meet. Thinking about Ralphie, a.k.a. Dogface, and others like him with similar backgrounds, I can't help but wonder why or how these children who grew up in households with loving parents, homes that were not lacking in material comforts, their parents provided them with all the electronics, toys, gizmos, and whatever tickled their fancies. They were never hungry, they attended good schools, had great friends, had the support of the entire family, never saw or heard their parents fighting, drinking, swearing, or using curse words. They were raised with good guidance and counseling, did not lack any attention, by all means they had lives that others not as privileged as them would be envious of, yet for some reason, they took to the streets as if pulled by some sort of invisible magnet of which they had no control. I call it the "the pied piper lure."

In stark contrast, there are children who grew up in orphanages, abandoned by their parents, totally unwanted, totally underprivileged, but they set themselves goals and turned out to be successful and brilliant.

ELLA

In our nineties, our species have completely or almost slowed down. We tend to move much slower than before. We talk less, chose our words more carefully, and have a mostly quiet demeanor. We come to terms with the reality that we have seen the faces of the years, that time changes and have changed everything, and we cannot travel back in time to rewrite the past or change the events or things we have experienced. Events and experiences have carved and fashioned our characters, have steered and influenced our way of life, our thinking and our destiny.

Not exactly the case for Ella Stein. She firmly refuses to give in or give up. In her mind, at the young age of ninety-six, why should she? Ella is another of the forerunners in this hi-rise building. She is a sharp-minded, gutsy, and feisty little woman. She knew almost everyone in the complex and everyone knew her. She knew details about the lives of practically all of her neighbors, much more than they would have imagined. Most of what she knew about her neighbors came to her straight from the mouth of Dogface.

Before she moved into the building, Ella lived in one of the most affluent neighborhood in an upscale town in Connecticut. She lived in a thirteen thousand square feet mansion and was surrounded by opulence and splendor. Her husband was a man without a collage education and was also a high school dropout who made his way through life by hustling, befriending the right people and also a few of the wrong ones.

Ella spoke of meetings, parties, and social gatherings at her house where she hosted many influential people, who brought them money-making proposals and connections. Unfortunately, too many of those opportunities went bad.

They were forced to sell their house for a lot less than it was worth; the situation was so desperate that the whole ordeal was too much for her husband to handle. The realization that with all of the hustling, wheeling, and dealing all of his life, and now in his later years everything has crumbled, cars repossessed, a house that was in danger of foreclosure, so-called friends abandoning him, this all came together and gave him a mental shock so great that he suffered a fatal heart attack.

And so it was that Ella took whatever money they had stashed here and there and a little she managed to squeeze out of some of his business dealings and bought a unit in this hi-rise complex.

The mansion, cars, and connections were gone, but the opulent mind-set stayed with her. She moved in with what was left of the artworks, fine china glassware, silverware, and furniture. She also brought with her the well-to-do attitude.

In the building, she was queen, belle of the ball. With her attitude, everyone thought of her as the richest person in the building, and she played her roll well. She reveled in it.

One of her greatest pleasures was when she would coax other residents into coming up to her apartment to view her china, figurines and needlework. Each Thanksgiving and Passover, she would decorate her table with china and silverware, and even though she was alone, the table would be laid out as if she was having at least a dozen guests over for a feast, as if trying to relive and recapture those glorious days at her mansion.

In addition to her well-to-do attitude, Ella had a mouth on her, a sharp tongue. She holds nothing back. Whatever she thinks or feels about you, she'll say it, even when what she concludes is inaccurate. Ella, in her conversations, has no hesitation in using the f—— word along with other expletives.

She, at her age, was very outspoken and critical about issues in the building and also issues regarding the residents, the condo association, and the management company. She had no kind words, praises, or credit for the condo board members or any of the various companies that managed the building over the years.

Her firm opinion is that they are all no-good bums who are there in their positions or capacities to filter funds into their pockets and set themselves up for kickbacks from contractors.

She made it her point of duty and her sense of purpose to keep abreast of the operation of the building, unlike a huge number of the residents and owners in this hi-rise community who prefer to be low key, live a quiet and peaceful life, and avoid the politics of the building, the perpetual gossiping, and the gossipers that abounds in this, and I would imagine that the same exists in all types of community living.

Ella was not the quiet type. She wanted to be in the know and to be one up on everyone in the building. She knew who all the gossipers were and was not afraid to call them out and wax sarcasm with them.

Whenever there is construction or repairs being done on the common areas of the building, this little old lady could be seen, with her hunched back leaning on her cane, loitering around the job sites, questioning the workers, and at times trying to tell them what to do, how to do a better job, and also acting like an inspector. Needless to say, these workers naturally get annoyed, but with the awareness that Ella is just a little old lady, they try their best to ignore her.

Once she came to the desk and asked me if I knew how many units in the building were occupied by renters. I answered, saying, "Gee, I don't really know, but if you really want to know and if you have the time, I will try to help you to figure it out." She went away after telling me to "hold on. She will be back in a couple of minutes."

Twenty or twenty-five minutes later, she returned with an over-sized sheet of paper with lines drawn to look like some type of chart. She placed it on the desk. I got up and offered her the chair. She sat down and beckoned me to begin telling her what I know in regard to the number of rented units.

After about thirty minutes of my trying to remember while informing her of what I could recall, and her filling in the slots on her chart, another resident (an elderly lady who had just been dropped off at the front door by her grandson) walked in.

While clutching on to her walker, she said, "Hi, Ella, how are you? Good to see you. You're looking so well. I wish I looked as good as you do. What are you doing?"

Ella replied, "I'm trying to make an up-to-date record of the correct ratio of rented units as opposed to the owner-occupied ones."

The other lady replied, "Great, that is a worthwhile and necessary project. I've always wanted to know. I think it will be good information for us owners."

"Yes," Ella said.

The lady responded, "May I have a copy of it when you are done?" Ella quietly nodded in affirmation. "Thank you," the lady said then slowly proceeded up the steps and around the corner toward the elevator.

Ella sat quietly looking at me while holding her pointing finger vertically against her lips, in the universal "shhhh" gesture, signaling me to be quiet and not speak, so that she would be able to hear the sound of the bell, signaling that the elevator door has closed and that it has moved away.

Ella asked, "Is she gone?"

I replied yes. At that moment Ella shouted, louder than any other ninety-six-year-old could, "WELL, FUCK HER! Who does she think she is? That bitch. I'm not her employee. She should go and do her own research."

With that said, she continued to fill in her chart, and after taking in all of that display of hypocrisy, I had no more desire to further help her with her task, so I lied when I told her at that point I didn't know of any other rented units.

Ella has three children, two daughters and a son. All three are grownups. The daughters live in different states and her son lives in a separate unit in this high-rise.

Her daughters rarely visit her. I have seen them on visits to her only a few times over the many years I've been here working as a doorman, and as you may already know how the saying goes, "Doormen see and know all the happenings in their buildings."

The girls do not come to see her on her birthdays, neither holidays or high holy days, even though they are a fully Jewish family.

For some reason, even her grandchildren are kept away from her. One granddaughter who defied her parents' wishes visited frequently in the past, but for whatever reason, that came to an abrupt end.

In her own words, Ella had told some, including myself, that her daughters visit her only when they want money or to talk her into giving them her antique items (pieces that they deemed valuable). When the money dried up and the antique pieces dwindled to a few, their visits also dried up and became too few to none.

The rumor in the hi-rise building is that the money dried up because it was all used up to support her son who lives in an apartment a couple of floors above her unit.

Her son who is about fifty-eight years old had not worked for the past twenty or more years due to (he claimed) injuries he suffered when he lifted and carried around heavy golf bags during the years he caddied for the big shots his father befriended. By lying around doing nothing but eat for twenty years resulted in him putting on the pounds, and now he can barely move his five hundred pounds body around, yet he continues to eat and eat and eat.

The people who deliver food to the building all know him because of their frequent visits to that unit making deliveries. At times as many as three pizza deliveries from different outfits checks in at the desk for permission to go up to deliver their orders, all within the span of six to eight hours.

No restaurant menu in this city has been left unordered, no matter the ethnicity or the size of the establishment, they, at some point in time, have delivered food to that specific unit in this high-rise, and for those establishments that don't offer delivery service, he will pay anyone who is willing and able to go and pick up the order for him, and oftentimes, it would be the doorman.

Due to his absolute inactivity, this son, this soul whom Ella loves so dearly, has numerous physical ailments and complaints, so many that inside his medicine cabinet resembles a mini drug store. If there is a hidden soft spot in Ella, a tender, forgiving, compassionate, kind spot, a weak spot, here is where you will find it, laying in the lap of her son.

His main and perhaps only form of exercise was when she would accompany him to the pool, then she would watch as he waded around in the shallow end, but this form of activity ended because Ella had determined that there was too much urine in the pool. Her take on this is that the swimming pool at this high-rise is not heated. Therefore, the water almost always have a chill factor (almost always chilly), and when individuals enter the water for the first few seconds, that initial chill hits the body's nervous system, and the body involuntarily lets out a little urine.

She contends that it happens more often with older folks, and she added that this is only a half of the fact. The other half are the people who gets into the pool, swimming, splishing and splashing, and having fun and are just plain lazy to get out to go to the bathroom, so they just conveniently pee then and there in the pool.

She explained that she is not guilty of conveniently peeing in the pool, but she has in the past experienced the chilly water effect and had felt the initial shock, which forced the urine out of her.

Seeing Ella and her son together, one may find it hard to believe that this little old lady who is ninety-six years old, under five feet in height, with spindly arms and legs, the hair on her head as white as a cloud, would be the protector, caregiver, and facilitator of this large man, who depended on her for everything for his very survival.

Ella's daughters refused to accept this situation. They felt that their brother, in his condition, should be placed in a nursing home facility, and that the situation and condition in which he found himself was all his doing. He brought this upon himself from being a lazy, good-for-nothing bum, who was not only killing himself, but also taking his mother down with him. For all of this, they despised him and blame her for facilitating and encouraging his lifestyle. They contend that from his younger years, his unproductive lifestyle has drained all the financial resources at hand and forced her to borrow from all the equities available, and now there is nothing left for them to inherit when she dies, and for that, they despise her too.

It is for this reason that the once-in-a-blue-moon times when they came to visit her, it was to see what items of any value are left (which haven't yet been sold) that they can grab for themselves before it is all gone.

As for us, the employees in the high-rise, Ella and her son showed a great degree of kindness. Speaking for myself, I can say that each time Ella went to buy groceries for herself and her son, she would pull her car up to the front door. For help in bringing the bags up, there would always be a separate bag for me filled with goodies from the higher-end health food stores (such as Baldacci's and Whole Foods) where she always buys her stuff.

The same goes for her son. Many times when I am on duty at the desk, when he called in his order for food delivery, he would often call me to ask if I wanted something to eat, and if the answer was yes, he would then go ahead and place an order for me also, and at the end of each year, at Christmas time, an envelope with a greeting card and money is always certain.

Although Ella was at an advanced age, because of her spunk, feisty, and lively spirit, it was totally unexpected when she began to fall while moving around in her apartment. At first, we noticed a little bruising on her arms and face, but when asked what had happened, she dismissed it, saying that she merely bumped into furniture. It then got worse. She started calling us to come up to help her up from the floor.

One day when she hadn't been seen or heard from, we went up to her unit and used the master key to get in, and there she was on the kitchen floor. We called 911. They came and took her to the hospital, where she was diagnosed with broken hip, rib, and leg bones. She was released from the hospital into a nursing home.

She never made it out of that home. About a month later, she died with only two people at her side, who throughout her ordeal, were the only ones who ever visited her, her son and myself.

NORA

There is one in every complex, every community, every project, every office, every neighborhood, and every high-rise, a busybody. There are varying degrees of these types of characteristics.

In this high-rise, Nora Alvaranga is at the highest degree. She is the queen bee of them all, the busybody of busybodies.

This characteristic has manifested itself in a pear-shaped, four feet eleven inches top-heavy, overweight frame called Nora.

She has the scoop on almost everyone in the high-rise; her mission is to know everything there is to know about every event and everybody.

One of her favorite places of gathering information and gossip is the lobby. She will show up at any given time, unexpectedly but mostly during the prime time hours of the day or evening when there is high foot traffic going back and forth through the lobby.

At the far left side corner of the lobby sits her favorite chair. She would take a seat in that chair and begin her questioning of the doormen, coaxing us to tell her all that we had seen and heard during the past week or month and also the latest hot gossip.

She is very aware that the lobby and the doorman's desk or round table is the epicenter, ground zero of the common areas, in this and/or any high-rise, a central point where all the resident's concerns, complaints, demands, requests, and all the gossips end up.

We are a prime source of her unquenchable thirst for the juicy stuff, and those among us who are willing to entertain her are her best friends and her favorites whom she often reward by bringing ziplock bags containing bits of goodies, such as nuts, candies, trail mix, and the like.

Other things she brought down are over-ripened fruits, and some of the things she offered are either stale, expired, or on the verge of going bad, most of which ends up going down the trash chute.

On special occasions, she would bring plates of food that she prepared from scratch of which all goes down the chute, but before we throw it out, we would uncover it and take a good, long look to carefully inspect it to determine what is in it, because later, when Nora returns to collect her dishes, she would always ask (something like), "How did you like the food? Did you like the beans, and how about the mashed potatoes? Did you like the chopped onions sprinkled over the asparagus, and what did you think about the gravy? Didn't it taste wonderful with garlic powder in it?"

We would reply, "It was very tasty. The asparagus was very tender, and oh! It was splendid the way you combined the rice with walnuts."

I think she asks these questions just to check if we threw the food out. She once gave a huge platter that she prepared specially for a former employee who was fired for bad conduct. After taking the plate, he waited and listened to hear the sound of the bell as the elevator closes, then he took it to the chute, and down it went. Remembering that she hadn't collected her mail, she returned ten minutes later, saw him, and asked, "How was the food?"

He replied great, but in her mind, she was saying, "How could he have eaten it so fast? Did he inhale it down?"

Right away she suspected that he threw it out, then in her usual manner asked, "How did you find the meatballs? Did you think the sauce was too thick?" knowing well that none of what she had just mentioned was on the plate; she stood there awaiting an answer.

He paused, hesitated for several seconds, then replied, "Wonderful, very tasty indeed. Where did you learn to cook so well?" Upon hearing his response, her first thought was to call him out on his lie, but instead, she gazed at him, shook her head, and walked away; food was never again offered to him by her since that day.

Little did she know that we are all guilty of throwing her offerings out.

We throw most of her offerings out because we've all (at some point) been in her apartment and saw how deplorable it was, to the point where it looked extremely unclean and unhealthy.

We, the doormen, came to the conclusion that her unit is and has always been in this condition because she is so preoccupied with other people's business, so busy being a busybody that she has no time to take care of her own business; therefore, she has no time to clean. She is so involved in the dirt of others that she failed to see her own.

Being the busybody that she is, the time and energy she spends trying to get all the news and gossip about her neighbors, their families, relatives, and guests, 95 percent of her waken hours is spent thinking about or trying to milk the gossip out of others who are willing to entertain her, and even the ones who are not.

When Nora sleeps, she dreams about gossip and gossiping; there is one doorman among us who is her favorite, her facilitator, divulger, entertainer, and main source of the latest news and gossip of the day.

Hence, his nickname "The Mouth," an appropriate name that the superintendent of the building bestowed upon him due to his loose tongue. He tells her everything she wants to know, and when he runs short of gossip, he fabricates it in order to please her; he thrives on gossip and rumors almost on the same level as she does.

When she comes to the lobby to take a seat in her favorite spot, with him on duty, it is like marital bliss in gossip heaven, and the lobby becomes their earthly haven.

So there she will sit on her favorite chair, spewing out questions, with him responding in like manner.

She wants to know who in the building is sick and with what type of sickness, and if so, were they taken to the hospital? Were they admitted? And who from the building went to visit them?

"Who is the lady that came to visit Tom, who lives on the second floor? This is her third visit. I've noticed he's been living here for seven years now without female visitors. I was of the impression that he was gay."

"Have you seen Mrs. Matthews from the seventh floor? I heard that her husband got too friendly with their cleaning lady who is from Ecuador. I was told that he left Joyce, moved in with her, and has filed for divorce."

"The word is that they both are now vacationing in Florida, with plans to get married in the future, in order for her to acquire legal status here. I heard that Mrs. Matthews is beyond consolation and pissed off in the worst way."

"Can you imagine Doris Perkins from the fourth floor? She just buried her husband only six weeks ago, and now she already has a boyfriend. I wonder where she found him. The poor guy looks like he's about to fall apart. He's limping so much. I doubt that he will last much longer."

"She might be burying him very soon also, though yesterday when I pressed the button on the elevator to go up to my floor, the elevator came down from the fourth floor, and when the doors opened, there was Doris and her limping boyfriend, smooching in the elevator. When they saw me, they were so startled, not realizing that the elevator had already reached the first floor, so they quickly straightened up, pretending that they were just merely standing there. I can't help but wonder if a certain part of his anatomy also limps."

"She is no youngster herself, but maybe she is with him because he may have money stashed away, which he will give to her."

During her seemingly endless prattling, the doorman (a.k.a. the Mouth) was thoroughly engrossed in the idle talk, occasionally injecting his feedback, making sure she knew that she had his full attention.

She continued, "If Doris from the fifteenth floor needs a man in her life so desperately, she should do the same as Trudy from the tenth floor. When her husband passed away, she got herself a younger man, a stud muffin who not only made her happy in more ways than one. He was not one whom she would likely be burying anytime soon."

"Good for her," the Mouth replied. "And did you hear that Fred Clark lost his job? Yes, he got laid off. The company he worked for is relocating. I wonder how he will be able to pay his maintenance charges. He is always at the resident's or association meetings, complaining that the common fees are too high and that he can no longer afford to live here in this high-rise."

"I once said to him, 'If you can't afford to live here, why do you stay? Why don't you move?' He hasn't spoken to me since."

"Do you remember the eldest son of the Higgins from the third floor? He had left for college about eleven years ago. Before he left, there were rumors going around that he was gay. I heard that he has moved back into the apartment with his parents and that he has AIDS. They say he looks very skinny and frail. It is said that he confines himself in one room in the apartment, because he doesn't want to be seen in the condition he's in, and his parents? They are hush-hush about the whole thing."

"I heard that Mrs. Harris in the apartment next to mine had the police here last week to arrest her grown son. Can you believe this guy? He's forty-six years old, living at home with his mother, does not have a job, has no intention of looking for one, has no skills, and sits around all day like a lazy bum."

She disclosed to me a few months ago that he contributes nothing to the household, not even a penny to help with the utility bills or food, but he likes to smoke weed, and on that day when the police came and took him away, he got into a heated argument with his mother, when she refused to give him the money he wanted and asked for to purchase some weed from his regular supplier who was anxiously waiting at the corner.

She had to eventually obtain a restraining order against her own son, in order to keep him away from the apartment and also away from her.

Having the full attention of the Mouth, Nora continued, "Did you get complaints about the party animals on the fifteenth floor? They were at it again last Saturday night. I heard that they had a real wild one as usual."

"They had far too many people in the apartment. The noise level was so high that their neighbors all around were so upset. They had had enough of those guys breaking all the rules they promised to adhere to when they moved into the apartment."

"The noise and ruckus did not come to an end when they were told by the doorman on duty that the owner would be fined by the association. Only when a neighbor threatened to call the cops to shut it down, did the noise eventually stopped."

"Although the noise stopped, it was strange that no one was observed leaving the apartment. It was not until four to five hours later when they started to trickle out one or two at a time, and during those hours, apart from an occasional giggle, it was mostly silent. There was no further disturbance to the surrounding units."

"One rumor in the building has it that after the partying was forced to stop, they resorted to one great big orgy in the apartment that night."

"And oh, you must have heard the news. Byron who lives on the sixteenth floor is about to lose his apartment to foreclosure. I heard he hasn't paid his mortgage, common charges, or property taxes for over three years, and now they are all going after him."

"He had been stalling them with stories of hardship, but those claims used by him for so long and so often have now been exhausted. He is now looked upon by all of his creditors as the proverbial boy who cried wolf. They no longer believe him."

"The untold story or the truth is, since his estranged wife walked out on him, he's been very busy dating other women in an effort to prove to her and himself that he can and will get someone who will be better than her in every way.

"Unfortunately, his efforts backfired. The women he has dated to this point were all gold diggers with only money and a good time on their minds."

"The poor guy was blinded in his quest for companionship and love. He poured out not only his heart and soul to those women, and he also poured out his time, energy, resources, and bank account, trying his hardest to impress them."

"He showered them with exotic vacations, fine dining, jewelries, loans, gifts, and more. He eventually went broke from living above his means. When they discovered that all his money was gone, they all took their bows and made their exits."

This is how Nora operates when she takes her seat in the lobby. The business and affairs of her neighbors and others just rolls off her tongue like a well-oiled machine.

An Eastern philosopher wrote, "Our worse fault is to preoccupy ourselves with other people's faults." He also wrote, "Empty heads have long tongues."

Nora aptly epitomizes these quotes; the question is, with individuals like Nora, how did they get to be the way they are? What kind of self-satisfaction is derived from spreading or indulging in gossips and rumors? Are they so bored in their own lives that they need to be entertained by the dilemmas of others? Is there a degree of this type of disposition in us all?

For individuals like Nora, I call it an obsessive compulsive disorder.

"He who knows not and knows not that he knows not is a fool, shun him.

He who knows not and knows that he knows not is a child, teach him.

He who knows and knows not that he knows is asleep, wake him.

He who knows and knows that he knows is wise, follow him."

—An Eastern Proverb

NOEL
(MR. KNOW-IT-ALL)

In our lives, we have all encountered, if not quite a few, at least one, an individual or individuals who acts as if they know everything, pretends to know everything, or thinks that they know everything.

The case in this high-rise is Noel. Upon listening to him, one will get the perception that he personifies the statement "Mr. Know-It-All."

With an almost-perfect posture, which exudes a feeling of strength—a strong, sure, and steady stride that gives the feeling of confidence; salt-and-pepper hair, with the bulk of the salt or gray concentrated at the temples, which portrays a feeling of wisdom, akin to the "wise old owl."

For a guy in his late seventies, he seemed to be in pretty good shape, and if he's not in the shape he appears to be in, he tries to enhance that appearance by being sharply dressed at all times. To be casually dressed is alien to him.

When it comes to fashion, he defies the term "when you are in Rome, do as the Romans." If the task he has to undertake is to dig a ditch, unclog a drainpipe under his kitchen sink, or to give Rex a bath, he would still be well dressed, at three in the morning or three in the afternoon. You won't find him otherwise. It would not come as a surprise to find out that he goes to sleep well dressed in a suit and shiny dress shoes, or maybe he has special designer sleepwears designed to look like double-breasted suits and tuxedos.

Though always dressed as sharp as a tack, he's never to be seen wearing modern styles, cuts, or trends due to his age and the era in which he grew up. His look and style is distinctly retro. His preferred neckwear is the bowtie (as opposed to the necktie).

Judging by the styles and types of materials he favors, it is evident and plain that he is stuck in the decades of sixties and seventies. His wardrobe is filled with clothes he had kept and saved over the decades, or it could be that he had a tailor who catered to clients of his persuasion, sort of like pimps, and the disco-era diehards who has all their attire of that era stashed away, just in case of a resurgence or a rebirth of that era, then they will be all set and ready to emerge from the woodwork.

Noel and others of the same mind-set truly believes in the saying "what goes around comes around" especially in the world of fashion and fads.

Although it has never been seen, displayed, or proven, he claims to be an expert in martial arts. Often times during a conversation (of which there were many), if the subject of personal safety should arise, he will make quick hand gestures of how he would subdue his attacker or attackers, most of which, to anyone who knows anything or even just a little bit about martial arts, would plainly see that what he was saying and doing was merely nonsense or bull crap.

Whatever the subject matter, be it a question, argument, debate, or dispute, he has in his opinion not just an answer or answers but the right answer or answers. Without acknowledging or denying it, his demeanor shows that he thinks that his word is and should be final.

In subtle ways, he feels that he's the authority on whatever is being discussed, and at certain times, especially late at night during the second shift, when there is little or no traffic in or out through the lobby, when most of the residents are in slumber land, a number of night hawks (males) who are either bored, are insomniacs, single or want to get away from their wives for whatever reason, or smokers who are not allowed to smoke in their apartments by orders from their wives will venture down to get their midnight fix.

When they get to the lobby front desk or round table, the subject matters discussed were numerous, varied, and seemingly endless. On different nights, the topics discussed may range from two, three, or four. The number of night hawks would also range between two, three, or four, usually myself, Noel, Heinrich, and another nighthawk.

The topics mostly discussed are religion, world wars, Hitler, world leaders, politics, economy, stock market, refugees, weather, automobiles, women, current affairs, world affairs, the state of the United States, and the management of this high-rise.

At the helm of any given topic is Noel, the (so it appears) master, guru, and officiator. Any event brought forward within any topic he already has a vast knowledge of the event and proceeds to give the details, where, if a fact check is done, most of his arguments and details would surely be inaccurate. Any state, city, or town named in America he has either lived, visited, or have conducted some sort of business there in the past.

Mention the weather and he will give you the history of what the weather was like when he was growing up and how different it is now; then it would end eventually with him acting as a weather forecaster, forecasting what he predicts the seasons will be like, in terms of severity or mildness for the next ten years.

It is truly amazing to all of us why Noel isn't as rich as Warren Buffet, because he is (according to his words and actions) a stock market wizard. He claims to know the market inside and out. He tries to impress us with stock market terminologies and jargons, such as *short, put options, charts, margins, forex, commodities, futures, Bollinger bands*, and more.

To most of us at the round table, all of these fancy and technical words are like a completely different language. He will boast about his trades, his trading plans and techniques. Due to our ignorance regarding this subject matter, we had no idea regarding accuracies or inaccuracies. In his boasting and fancy talk, he would only shut up when we asked him, "You've been involved in the market and trading for forty years. You claim to be an expert. How come you haven't gotten rich?"

He sometimes will respond, saying, "Oh! My moment hasn't arrived yet. I am still waiting for the gigantic crash, when there is 'blood in the streets." Then and there I will risk my all, make a killing, and be rich beyond words."

"And just what will you do with all that money at your age with no children?" I would ask.

His response would always be the same. Smirking, he would say, "I will divorce my wife, move to Miami's south beach, buy a luxurious condo, and surround myself with scantily clad women."

On the subject of politics, he knows all. He knows the inner workings of the machine. He knows all about the cover-ups, the tricks, the deceptions, the criticisms, the dirt, the mud-flinging, and the ever-so-vital lies, which every politician knows that he or she has to do, because it comes with the turf.

Noel added, "If you are afraid to lie, then stay away from politics. You will never fit in." He told us that he knows these thing firsthand because he twice ran for political positions. Once for a city council seat and another time for state representative. Of course he, Noel, could also very well be lying.

When the topics of world leaders and world affairs were brought forward and being discussed, he had all the answers to all the ills and conflicts that plague the world. To him, most, if not all, of the world leaders are incompetent idiots, especially the ones who open their borders and take in thousands of refugees. "That's just asking for trouble," he contends.

He is certain that if it were in his hands, he would do a better job of bringing order in this world, much better than those so-called prime ministers, presidents, kings, princes, and strongmen and dictators.

In many of the late-night, front desk or roundtable talks, during, or after a discussion on almost any subject, the topic of law and laws would eventually take over, and while we guessed and pondered whether a certain situation or action would be within the framework or contrary to the law, Noel would set things straight.

He professes that he knows all aspects of law and jurisprudence; he would proceed to dominate the conversations with what we guessed as legal verbiage and terminologies, which reminded us of a Long Island railroad shooter and mass murderer, who after shooting several of the passengers, at his trial, decided to defend himself by acting as his own attorney; and in the courtroom, he played the part of lawyer so well, his poise and gestures would make Perry Mason or Johnny Cochran envious.

When asked where he acquired his vast knowledge of the law, Noel proceeded to tell us that he studied law as a younger man but later dropped it due to a multitude of other interests. When he said that, we all looked at each other and smiled. We already knew what the answer would be. The smile is also a "lest we forget" reminder that Noel knows everything.

On one of the most complicated of all subjects ever to be discussed at the lobby desk (and universally, I would imagine), again Noel knows all, all about women or the opposite sex, our better half, the prettier half, the fairer half, the boss—however you refer to women. Noel claims he has them figured out—the way they think, why they say the things they say, why they act the way they act, why they do the things they do, and what they think about men.

He has all the answers. In this case we had no reason to doubt him, because whatever is asked of him, whether it's to go fishing with us, to put a dollar in the lottery pool, or to have a beer with us, anything, his answer would be, "I would like to, but first I have to ask my wife."

THE WOMEN

In this high-rise lives quite a few older individuals who are beyond taking care of themselves. These people hire caregivers or aides and companions to assist in getting them through their days and nights also because many of those residents require twenty-four hours of care.

The people hired to assist them are women, mostly from countries like Haiti, Poland, Jamaica, and Eastern Europe. These women spend long hours taking care of the elderly residents in the building. There are those who are here with their cases as live-in caretakers and companions.

We the doormen got to know them very well, and whenever they had some free time or on trips to the pharmacy, they at times stop at the front desk to talk to us. The ones who live in are mostly single while others with spouses and children would occasionally pull overnighters; these are the ones with grown children who sometimes welcome the break from their husbands (so they tell us.)

The long and sometimes boring hours these "live-ins" endure while living with and caring for these older folks, some of whom barely speak or move, eventually instills in these ladies, a silent thunderous longing, a longing to engage in face-to-face conversations with others. It is for this reason that they come to the lobby desk to speak to us as often as they possibly can, because they know that we are always there, ready to give a listening ear.

I can only assume or guess that after these ladies have tucked the older folks in for the night (which is usually between seven and eight) thereafter, they have a huge amount of down time, and when they get tired of watching the television, the longing sets in.

This longing eventually turns into desires, then deeper desires; I say this because quite often, I would get a phone call at the front desk in the wee hours of the night, usually between twelve thirty and one, and it would be one of the caretakers or companions, calling to ask if I could spare a minute to come up to check something that was not working. Sometimes it is a light switch, an outlet, a leaky faucet, a toilet that doesn't flush, or it could be any of a long list of things.

Upon venturing up to the unit, knocking gently on the door so as to not awaken the sleeping elderly person, the door would slowly open, and upon entering, my eyes would behold a scantily clad woman beckoning me to come in, and once inside the apartment, she would quietly move around not trying to cover up or hide anything. When walking ahead of me as she showed me the item she called me about, the very same item, which is supposedly not working, upon checking I found that the thing that she called me about is working fine, and it was quite clear that it was working fine all along.

Sometimes I would be asked, "Would you like to have a cup of coffee or tea while you're here?" It is said that action speaks louder than words, and from her actions, in my mind, I could clearly hear the words, "Take me, please!" And she continued to quietly flex her attributes while pretending to not purposely doing so. Sipping from the cup of tea that I accepted, she would invite me to sit for a few minutes and have the tea.

We sat on the couch with her sitting at one end. She throws one leg over the arm of the sofa and the other leg positioned in such a way that nothing was left for the imagination. Being in a dimly lit room along with a fairly attractive woman wearing nothing but a short see-through sleepwear with no underwear, sitting, walking, and standing in suggestive ways will awaken even the most dormant, hidden, or forgotten carnal desire in any man, which was what happened in my case.

At that moment, my sipping went more rapidly in an effort to finish the tea faster. Then I stood up, thanked her for the tea, and reluctantly told her that I must return to my duty at the front desk.

If there are any perks that comes with being a lowly doorman, maybe it's these bored women whose jobs taking care of the elderly become so mundane, and being stuck in the apartments with an older person who retires to bed at seven o'clock after a day of loving care given them by these ladies. They then have long evenings ahead of them. Then as the night rolls on and with no one else to talk to, they know that we are always there at the lobby desk or round table.

I can't speak for the other guys or doormen, but as for me, I get these calls quite often. I can recall times when I had gone up to help with one thing or another, and in the process, I would get suddenly and unexpectedly a big wet kiss smack dab on the lips. It would be so unexpected I would momentarily freeze from not knowing what to do or how to react in that situation.

Then there were times when I would be called up to look at a problem in the living room, and during the process I would hear, "Can you also take a look at the air conditioning unit in my room? It's not cooling properly." And if it happens to be winter it would be, "Can you take a look at the heating unit in my room? I am not getting enough heat."

When I got to the room, she would be butt naked, moving about or reclining as if she is alone in the room, occasionally glancing at me to see my reaction to her, in all her glory. Each time she glanced at me, it just so happened to be the same time I would be taking a look at her assets.

The temptation of the flash is very strong, more so when a body is in good shape and well proportioned. These women had this type of body, so stared I did. But fear prevented me from ever taking it farther than the point of lust.

Each time these events took place, right at the boiling point, I would interrupt the mood and distract myself and the lady by saying something like, "The air conditioner seems to be working fine and I should hurry back to my work station."

Once in the elevator, on my way down to the lobby, I couldn't stop wondering what the lady must be thinking, then I would imagine her saying to herself, "This guy has to be gay. He's a gay fucker. He is as gay as they come."

Occasionally, I would get calls from female residents who wanted me to apply either body lotion or other medicated ointments on their backs. A very friendly older lady in her mid to upper eighties once called me to help with closing a difficult-to-close window in her dining room. On the dining table, I noticed photo albums covering the entire surface as if she was sorting through photographs and in the same process looking at pictures of herself in her much younger days and probably reminiscing about the joys and gaiety of her youth.

I could not help but notice the picture of a stunningly beautiful, drop-dead, knockout young woman wearing a sexy bikini. I asked her, "Who is that gorgeous woman?"

She replied, "That's me!"

I responded with a wow. Again, she replied, "Look at that body. Isn't it something, and I still got it. I still have that same-looking body even to this day. I never lost it!" Upon hearing that, I naturally gave her a quick head-to-toe and toe-to-head gaze.

Being aware of my gaze she responded, saying, "Would you like to see it?" As she proceeded and unzip and unbutton my response was quick.

I replied, "No, no, no," and at the same time being diplomatic, when I continued, "You don't have to take anything off. Even with your clothes on, I can clearly see that you haven't lost it."

Another time when I was called by one of the most attractive and sexiest woman anyone can imagine, she was a younger woman in her late twenties with long black hair, a golden tanned skin, a beautiful face, a slender, well-proportioned, trim, and sexy body.

A bat had entered her unit through an open window. It was flying around in circles in her bedroom, and she was apparently so frightened by and scared of the creature that she bolted out of the room, slammed the door shut, so the bat would be confined to that room only, and ran quickly to the phone to call the front desk for help. But by moving so fast and being so scared she forgot that she had on only her G-string underwear and nothing on top. So when she opened the door to let me in (using biblical language to describe what I saw), I beheld the fullness thereof, and I felt my cup runneth over with desire and lust.

She was so shaken that the thirty plus minutes I spent speaking to her and eventually catching the bat, during all that time she perhaps didn't realize or didn't care that she was almost naked; she was relieved that the bat was removed. And my eyes and senses had a feast that night.

In this high-rise, I've always gotten and returned friendly and pleasant smiles from some of the residents and guests, like this young lady who very often visits her mother, which I told her was very admirable because there are many residents living in this high-rise (especially the older ones) who rarely, or never get a visitor, not even their own children.

This particular young woman would give me the most pleasant of smiles, and along with the smile came a gaze that would last a bit longer than the norm. Those pleasant smiles eventually turned into brief conversations, which eventually turned into longer ones, in which she would indirectly suggest a different venue to have these talks. For example, she would ask, "What do you do when you are not working here?"

I would respond with a vague answer, "Oh, I keep myself busy," and it never went farther than that.

One rainy and chilly night, she came to visit her mother, and as usual, the pleasantries went back and forth between us. She then went up to see her mother.

A couple of hours later, she came down to talk, and so we did. The lobby front desk is flanked by two columns. She stood with her back leaning against the column on the right. With the chair at the desk being a swivel type, I could easily turn to face her if necessary.

On that evening in particular, she wore a loose knee-length dress. While talking to her, I saw her taking quick looks to the left, then right, and all around, and when there was no one in sight, she said, "Take a look at what you are missing out on," then with her back against the post, she lifted her dress. She had no underwear on. She held it up for about five seconds to reveal a neat, thick patch of pubic hair, nestled between a pair of silky smooth thighs.

It was an amazingly beautiful sight to behold; it was so unexpected that for those five seconds, I froze while looking at her womanhood. When I regained control, I quickly grabbed the skirt and pulled it back in place while saying, "Oh my god, you are so lovely, but you can't do this here."

She smiled at me and said, "Now it's up to you," then she left.

CHUCK

If there is such a thing as a genuinely good person, if you think all the honest ones among us are all gone, leaving only the bad and rotten ones, or if you know for sure that there isn't a soul left here on earth with a good nature, a kind heart, a person with pure thoughts, and goodwill toward his fellow human brothers and sisters, most people reading this will immediately think of, or associate these characteristics with Jesus Christ, the prophet Mohamed, Gautama Siddhartha, Gandhi, Mother Theresa, or the Dalai Lama, all of whom had in their hearts a deep and sincere love for humanity.

In this high-rise lives a person who comes close to the personification and manifestation of these characteristics: a good-natured man with a humble disposition, a gleeful spirit, and a beautiful soul.

From my observation, he puts his heart and soul into whatever good deed he does for others. It is said that "the nice guy finishes last," but if a person gives freely of him or herself—his advice, his word, his thoughts, his assistance, his guidance, and material belongings to the needy. For this type of person who has no demands, does not expect rewards, someone who readily welcomes constructive criticisms, who is not looking for reciprocations, praises or recognition, it matters not if he or she finishes last.

Chuck (Charles Waters) is this type of person, a humble soul who readily greets everyone with a smile on his face; I would not be surprised if I am told that even if he saw a ghost, the smile would still stay on his face.

We all know that no one is perfect, and of course, Chuck is certainly no exception to the rule. It's just that if there is a flaw, it is cleverly hiding somewhere inside or behind his persona.

But I simply haven't been able to see it. Maybe someday this negative spot will eventually show its ugly face, but at this point in time, we can only comment on what we see before us, and that is a kind and virtuous human being.

Arguably, there is a lot of truth in the saying "The wisdom that a wise man tries to communicate always sounds foolish in the ears of the majority." In Chuck's case, many people in this high-rise building thinks he is a nutcase. In their minds, and what they are saying is, "How can anyone in this fast-pace, high-stress rat race of a society maintain such calm?"

He doesn't smoke, doesn't hit the bottle, doesn't swear, is not on weed or any kind of heavy shit, so how does he take the edge off? This invisible sword we call stress, which in our so-called modern societies, is always positioned like a snake, ready to strike, a psychological effect that renders us perpetually on edge.

We know that this edge has gotten the better of us when we lose our composures, unable to control our angers and attitudes, or when we get nervous breakdowns. Mr. Waters, in his own way, unlike the rest of us seem to have gotten the better of that edge. He seems to be one up on it at all times.

A neighbor of his, a lady who has lived in this high-rise for many years and recently lost her son to cancer, relayed to me that after her loss, she sank into a deep depression, where she was angry at life, angry at herself, angry at the world, and angry at God. She told me, she was at a point where she felt as if she did not want to go on living anymore. She asked herself, "What is the purpose of this life anyway, if from the moment of birth we begin a journey to death, a journey filled with complexities, a journey in which the interludes of joy and happiness are fleeting?"

After clawing our way through this existence, and along the way gathering the material stuff of the world around us and desperately believing in and clinging to religious and spiritual beliefs and dogmas, which provides very little answers, and in some cases leads to more confusion, after her great loss, she concluded that life is pain, and then we die.

Her head was filled with these thoughts and questions of which there were and are no answers, and with the lack of answers, she sank even deeper into depression and confusion. She relayed to me that Chuck had brought her back from a threshold of gloom and doom. There were days, she said, that she was in such deep sorrow that she would find herself crying for half of the day, and most of the other half she spent staring into nothingness. It got to a point where she often thought about checking out, out of this misery we call life.

So on that day after her crying spell was over, she stared at a bare wall that had become her nothingness. She had spent so much time staring unconsciously at that very wall, it was as if she saw right through it and found nothing on the other side.

She heard a knock on her door, which startled her out of the trancelike state she had been in, the result of staring at the wall for such long periods. When she opened the door and saw the figure of a man standing there with a pleasant smile on his face, for a few seconds, she swore she had seen the face of her son, smiling at her, which brought a brief moment of inner joy, happiness, hope, and a faint smile that slowly vanished when her thoughts cleared and she realized it wasn't him.

At that moment she burst into tears while saying to Chuck, "I am sorry, I am sorry," but Chuck was there to offer his condolences and support, and it wasn't surprising that he also became a comforter.

She described how her crying became uncontrollable. It was then that he held her hands, led her over to a chair, sat down, then directed her to sit on his lap, which she did, and there he cradled and comforted her till the crying stopped, her tears ebbed, and he kept on comforting her, and calmness fell upon her.

She also described how she felt as a grown woman being cradled and comforted. She felt as if she was a child again, being comforted by a parent. She felt the sincerity and total innocence in his actions.

When most of us either look the other way or just can't be bothered, Charles Waters tend to seek out situations where he can offer help in any way possible—a kind gesture, a helping hand, a comforting word, positive support, and encouragement. He's always ready, willing, and able. I can clearly remember a bitterly cold winter day.

There was a blizzard the night before and there was snow everywhere like mini mountains.

At this high-rise, like most condominium complexes, it is the duty of the maintenance staff to shovel and clear the snow from the driveways, walkways, and parking areas. This is one of the benefits of living in a condo. Residents are spared the labor of all external maintenance.

On that bitter day when the other residents were huddled on their couches, still in bed or looking out their windows at the winter wonderland from the coziness of their warm and balmy apartments sipping hot cocoa, coffee, or tea, Chuck had already grabbed a shovel and was out alongside the guys shoveling hand in hand with them. Even when told by the superintendent and porters to go back inside and keep warm, he refused, saying, "An extra pair of hands with a shovel gets the job done faster and easier."

It is not unusual to see Mr. Waters sitting and chatting with the homeless people who frequent the park benches and sidewalks in the downtown area of this city.

He got to know most of them through the voluntary work of bringing them donated food, which he does a few evening each week along with a small group of likeminded people. He once told me that some of these homeless people are sincerer, appreciative, and honest than most of his neighbors and so-called friends.

Another admirable voluntary gesture that Chuck undertakes is one that as a child I eagerly look forward to every Friday and Saturday evening. My brother, sister, cousins, and myself, along with other neighborhood children, would gather in our backyard in warm weather or in the family room if it was cold or raining.

We were always excited and eager as we set on little benches, on the floor, or outside in a patch of grass near the back door while we waited for our grandmother to emerge and begin her story telling, and even though we were noisy, talkative kids, once she began, we were silent and spellbound by the sometimes-pleasing, sometimes-dramatic, and sometimes-unexpected events in the stories she told, which ranged from fairytales to true-to-life events in her life, the lives of family members, people she met along life's path, from books she would read to us, or from books she read in the past.

At these gatherings, the readings and storytelling stimulated, enriched, and enlightened us in many ways, even to this day in our adult lives. In this fast-paced, electronic, computerized digital world in which we live today, my hope is that the children in the orphan homes were Chuck goes to read and do his storytelling will be just as enlightened as we are. This type of activity is necessary today because it brings back the humanity in our lives, which is needed in this era of ever-expanding artificial intelligence.

Chuck, in my opinion, is a person one could refer to as an earth angel, though there are those who would swear that he is from a place called flake city. These people will say this, because, unfortunately, in a society where it is mostly the bad and/or chaotic news and events captivates and holds our attention.

Whenever we encounter a person like Chuck who oozes kindness and brotherhood, we get confused and suspicious. It seems either we are not used to seeing constant kindness, or maybe, we don't want to see it. Unfortunately, the rotten, rotting, and negatives have become the mores of our so-called modern societies.

The kind and jolly gentleman who one day went around the city of Seattle handing out dollar bills to people he randomly approached as he greeted them, saying, "Life can be good, have a happy day, share a dollar" was only able to hand out a small number of bills.

Most of the people he tried to approach sidestepped him while saying something negative like "out of my way, you creep." The ones sitting in their cars quickly rolled their windows up after listening to his greeting.

When I heard the story about this gentleman, I immediately thought of Chuck. He is the type of person who will do this act of goodwill. He truly believes in the biblical verse "Do unto others as you would have them do unto you."

DAPHNE

We have, in our society, far too many of us who are frustrated, disappointed, and downright tired. We are frustrated with our jobs, commitments, and responsibilities. Disappointed with ourselves, our relationships, and just plain tired of playing the survival game, a game that has gotten stuck in a revolving mode of getting up and going to work, paying the bills, meeting deadlines, getting to appointments, trying hard to live up to expectations, trying to be healthy, and then we die.

In this high-rise, frustration abounds. It is evident on the faces of residents as they pass by us each day. Then there are those who do not just merely pass by. They stop at the lobby desk or round table to express their frustrations and vent their angers. We the doormen are the perpetual listeners. We try our best to not give too much input, but listen we do.

Just as we are perpetual listeners, there are those residents who are perpetual grousers who leave no stone unturned when they come to the lobby desk or round table. It is perhaps not evident to them that we are just as, if not more, frustrated than they are (and also with some of them).

Of all those who stop by to express their grouses, Daphne is the most upset and the most disappointed. She, a fairly attractive woman, fifty-five plus, well educated, with a PHD and various other degrees under her belt, she in the past has held a number of important and well-paid positions in jobs related to her field of studies, but for some reason, each and every position and job she held were short-lived. She blames it on the assumption that she was the victim of sabotages against her by people who (wherever she worked) were jealous of her good looks, accomplishments, and leadership qualities.

The truth and real reasons for her quick exits from those jobs are not known by those who know her, but they do know that for quite a while her efforts and quests to find a new job has not been fruitful, even with all of her qualifications.

She had on occasions hinted that her inability to land a job was due to her age. She is also aware of time slipping by ever so quickly, and the fact that as each year passes, it becomes harder to for her to gain employment.

My grandmother once told me that men usually get a few chances in their lives to be successful. If these opportunities are missed, they will most likely never come around again, and therefore, the man will struggle to make ends meet for the remainder of his life.

Women, on the other hand, have more options than men; she explained that if a woman missed her opportunities, she will most likely find a man of means who would be willing to take care of her; wherein, it is much harder for a man to find a woman of means who would be willing to take care of him.

Armed with the awareness of time hurrying by and cognizant of the fact that it also robs us of our firm features and good looks, Daphne has increasingly been giving hints about finding such a man who will rescue her from the web of uncertainty in the job market and the biased grip of the corporations in their ruthless dog-eat-dog society.

She remains hopeful that if all else fails, this chance will still be there, that hopefully, this man will have the means to take care of her financially and hopefully strong enough to appreciate and admire what little she has left of her once-firm features, in order for him to perform in bed and deliver some degree of sexual satisfaction.

Oftentimes at the lobby desk or roundtable, she would come to inquire about something simple, like her newspaper not delivered that day, which would turn into small talk, then into more in-depth conversations, and during those times, she would express her regrets about decisions she made in the past, about not having the courage to have lived her life differently.

She expressed that in hindsight, she would have done things differently and not have placed all the emphasis on her career and zero time or effort on building solid relationships, both platonic and intimate; she told of herself being like a machine, a robot, programmed to move along the straight and narrow, with all sensors focused at one point on the horizon, a journey in which the horizon seemed to move farther away as she kept on pushing forward in her dogged, desperate attempt to become financially successful.

She regrets not bearing a child, or for that matter "children." Now her child-bearing years are a distant past and she is alone. She spends her evenings reminiscing about the many suitable gentlemen callers that she had turned away, brushed aside, or laughed at their advances. She said that at this stage and point in her life, those advances have become few and far between, and the few in question are from lazy bums less than half her age, who are looking for desperate older women to trick into giving them whatever money they might have. Or old farts that are looking for a little action on the side, trying to convince themselves that they haven't lost their manhood after continuous failed attempts with their wives. They feel that someone new or a younger body will rejuvenate their long-lost libido.

Some of Daphne's past coworkers remember her as the bossy, opinionated type who, once hired, begins to take over, a know-it-all who bosses everyone around even her own boss.

They describe her as a force to reckon with; therefore, they were not surprised when they learned of her plight. They think of her as a hurricane or a tornado passing through, and that for any man to live with or be around her for any length of time, his life would be living hell. Only a saint or an angel would be able to tolerate her, and they hope that for her sake, time has changed her.

NELLIE

I once saw a movie that describes and depicts humans as takers, unlike other animals we share the planet with, who only kill to eat, and in doing so, they kill only what is needed or necessary, which allows Mother Nature to maintain its delicate balance.

The human animal on the other hand is depicted as a greedy contaminating virus or a pervasive and invasive weed, which continuously moves from place to place, killing or chasing away all that was already there. Slowly destroying the life-giving elements around us, we continue our march, leaving behind our poisonous wastes.

If ever there was an exception to the taker mentality, it would be Nellie Philpot; Nellie, at age eighty-seven, has lived in this high-rise for over twenty years. Her husband was a local judge who "I heard" showed no form of leniency when imposing sentences before striking his hammer. It is said that the reason for Nellie being the way she is now, is for her, a form of redemption for the many people her husband had sent to the slammer, people she deemed innocent.

Nellie was a giver, one of the most giving, kind, and generous person we will ever encounter; she is generous to a fault. If you should ever walk into her apartment, you would observe a very sparsely furnished space, so sparse, that when speaking, your voice would echo, as in an empty room, then you would think, "okay, this is her style and preference," but you will soon discover that it is really not what you thought.

The real reason why her place is 90 percent empty is because she had given away almost all of her belongings. Her apartment now only consists of the bare basics—a bed, a table with two chairs, a small bookshelf, a loveseat, a thirteen-inch tube television set, a stove, and a refrigerator. These are the items in her thirteen hundred square feet two-bedroom apartment.

There are very few pieces of clothing remaining in her closets. In the kitchen, cookware, china, silverware, glassware, all but the few remaining were given away. Even her valuables were not spared the fate of her giving hands. Silver, gold, and diamond jewelries were also given away.

Nellie's daughter, who controls her mother's money, would make available a certain amount of cash in hand along with money in a checking account each month for her mother to spend on the things she needs, but within the first week of each month, the monies allotted to her would be all gone. Given away of course! And who were the recipients of Nellie's generosity? You might ask, the answer is "no one in particular."

The recipients are mostly random individuals or groups. For example, an employee in the building who helps her to open a jar of pickles would be rewarded with a fifty-dollar bill. A handyman who fixes a lamp would be paid triple the amount he charged. The extras would be counted as a tip.

She gave to the lady who cleans for her quite a few pieces of high-quality furniture, fine china, and clothing. I once told her of a person I knew who was accepting clothing donations to be sent to the country of Haiti for victims of the devastating earthquake.

Nellie had the person over and then emptied her closets, giving all but the few pieces that she wears around the house. Along with the clothes, she gave all of what was left of the money her daughter had allotted her for that month. The depth and extent of her giving in many ways is either truly incredible or amazingly foolish.

She once called me to check why her gas range would not fire up. Upon checking, I found that it was simply the pilot light needed to be re-lit, yet she began to write me a check for two hundred and fifty dollars, which I promptly refused, and at that time, I asked her about her overly generous outlook on giving.

She began to tell me that during her over eight decades of living, she has observed the behaviors, patterns, and characteristics of us humans, and one of the most compulsive of our behaviors is our propensity to gather and store stuff around us.

This condition is especially true in the United States of America, the proverbial land of plenty. "During our lifetime," she continued, "we surround ourselves with things of all sorts, of which only a small percentage is absolutely necessary, and in time, we become attached to this stuff, then slowly we die surrounded by our stuff."

Nellie's contention is, she knows that some material things are necessary, but when our desire to keep wanting more and more things and eventually acquiring them, then we, in some ways, become slaves to our possessions due to the time, effort, and expense we put out in order to maintain and protect these possessions.

On the other side, when we don't have the means to acquire more stuff, we become envious of those who have more or better stuff than our stuff. In some cases, those without the means to acquire more possessions or stuff develop desperate ways and methods that involve stealing, lying, deceiving, and killing just to get more stuff.

She explained that by giving, she feels mentally and physically freer, lighter, and happier.

IRENE

There is a piece of artwork, a painting with a profound message. I have never stood before the original work itself, but each time I see a picture of it in a book or some other form, it penetrates the essence of my being, down to the core of my humanity. It was painted by Ivan Albright, an American artist. The title is "Into the world there came a soul called Ida."

This piece of artistic expression is insightful and intriguing. It holds a powerful message for all of us humans, and it is telling us that time, life, youth, and beauty are fleeting.

It depicts a seated woman looking into a mirror, gazing at a face that longed for beauty; she sits with a powder puff in her hand, held to her chest, possibly wishing there was a way to gain and preserve beauty and also to regain her youth.

Whenever I think of this artwork, this painting, and its mood, it reminds me of someone; it reminds me that, in this high-rise, there lives a soul called Irene.

Irene is a middle-aged Woman who is grossly overweight. *Obese* might be a more appropriate word when describing her weight. She had tried many diets, all of which promised timely and miraculous weight loss. In the end, zero weight loss was the result. At times, she would try to convince herself that she is actually losing weight when, in fact, not a single pound was lost.

Periodically, she would call the front desk to check if any packages were delivered for her. If the answer was yes, she would then ask me or whoever else is on duty to bring it up for her. She asked for this favor because, for her, walking was becoming increasingly difficult.

The excess weight she carried left her waddling when she tried to walk. Those times when I brought packages up for her, she would struggle to get up from the lazy boy or from a reclining position on the couch. And after minutes of trying, she would eventually stand upright. She would then ask me, "Did you see how much weight I've lost?" which puts me in an awkward situation and left me asking myself, "Should I lie and say yes, or tell her the truth which was no?"

I would get out of the situation by saying something like "Your determination is truly admirable," but even as she asked, I could not help noticing the almost-empty bag of potato chips, the empty cookie bag, and cookie crumbs all over and around the couch. Empty and not yet opened soda cans were also present on the floor around the couch.

Irene was totally inactive. She hadn't worked for the past decade due to a back injury she sustained on the job. Her inactivity had contributed greatly to more weight gain, and she had been living on her social security and workman's compensation benefits since then.

The money she gets pays her monthly expenses and for the numerous diet plans she invests in, and when they fail (which they always do), she gets frustrated and turns to junk food for comfort, as if she was saying to herself, "All that effort for nothing, what the hell! I might as well eat what I really want. I will never lose this weight anyway."

When thinking of Irene, it is hard to comprehend her lifestyle. She is really a gentle soul who is trying her best to be socially accepted and wanted. She craves the need to be desired so much that she uses her imagination to create her own reality.

On one occasion, she called the front desk to say, "I am expecting a visitor. His name is Trevor. Please allow him to come up to my unit when he arrives," but Trevor never arrived. Trevor was a figment of her imagination, and so was Frank, Cornell, Nick, Clyde, and others who we were told would be coming over.

Things got worse when she carried on an imaginary year-long relationship with a made-in-her-head boyfriend named Clark; there were "do not disturb" signs on her door and takeout food delivery persons delivered orders for two. She would ask us to secure a parking spot for him so that when he arrives, he wouldn't have the problem of trying to find parking.

During those imaginary visits, when walking in the hallway, one could hear voices engrossed in conversations, but listening more keenly would reveal one person speaking and acting out (perfectly), conversations between two people.

We, the doormen, believe that with her imaginary visitors, she would deliberately speak in elevated tones so that her neighbors passing by in the hallway would not think of her as someone living a forlorn existence. I remember clearly one of her imaginary episodes; it was about twenty-five minutes after a Chinese food delivery. I had gone up to her floor to give an elderly neighbor a prescription, which was dropped off earlier by the pharmacy delivery service.

Walking back to the elevator, I had to pass by her unit, and even when several feet away from the door, I could hear a lively conversation coupled with the clinking of cutlery. It was a conversation extolling the tastiness of the food.

I heard, "Clark, isn't this mixed vegetables dish absolutely delicious?"

"Yes, indeed," came the answer. "Oh, Irene, I'm really pleased that you insisted on the Kung Pow chicken. It certainly is tasty."

"Oh, Clark, I'm so glad you like it. It's my favorite, but your order of sesame shrimp is also very good."

"Thanks, Irene, but with so much food, I'm beginning to feel full. Maybe I had too much of the rice. I don't want to be too full. It may spoil my ability to get frisky with you later."

"Oh, Clark, you're such a dog." Then there was laughter, and as I continued to walk toward the elevator, the one person acting as two went on.

On a couple of other occasions, when I took packages up for her, there was a set for two dining table, adorned with candles, wine glasses and a bottle of wine, awaiting Clark's arrival.

One morning after she had asked us to assist Clark with a parking space the night before, an insensitive doorman who was on duty asked her, while she sat in the lobby awaiting a taxi to take her to a medical appointment, "How is Clark? How was your evening yesterday?"

"Oh, he's all right I guess," she replied. "He left early last night. He made me upset and I told him I needed to go to sleep early in order to prepare for my appointment this morning."

The doorman who asked about her evening with Clark was not the only insensitive comment aimed at Irene in this high-rise; her neighbors were overheard (many times), making negative and insensitive comments about her. Comments about her being overweight and obese were the most common; they also talked about her being lazy and without purpose. These were the same neighbors who, when they met her in the elevator, hallway, or elsewhere, would smile with her, chat with her, shower her with well wishes, and when she was out of sight, the same people would refer to her as fat ass.

Those insensitive hypocrites failed to see beyond her physical appearance, failed to see the person within.

If I were to describe Irene, I saw a bundle of hope, aspirations, goodwill, and pure thoughts, a person who desperately wanted to fit in, a person yearning to be physically admired, trapped in an overweight body. A body that she had tried desperately and unsuccessfully to transform.

Despite her inner beauty, her humanitarian outlook, her gentle demeanor and kind ways, she was well aware that society places a greater emphasis on physical appearance than inner beauty.

There had been many times when she felt the urge to just simply check out, out of the obese frame, which imprisoned her, but fear of the unknown prevented her from taking the ultimate leap.

She once told me that out of utter frustration, she joined a support group exclusively for overweight and obese people. She said that she thought being around people in the same position as her would make her feel better, because in her mind, she could not possibly be the largest person in the group, and seeing people larger than her would make her not feel as bad as she felt, but surely, that didn't work. Even though there were a few people there who were bigger than her, she told me she had to get out of there fast, because it was very discouraging being around all those fat people, herself included.

There was not much comfort getting away from the group and coming home to this high-rise. Each time she returned home, the thoughts entered her head. "Why me?" she thought. "Why am I the fattest person in this hi-rise building. Why couldn't I have been as thin as a reed? Why are my slender thought and feelings trapped in this oversized body? What would it feel like to have handsome men swooning around me, like moths around a flame? To be able to wear fancy dresses, skin-tight jeans, and itsy-bitsy bikinis?"

These thoughts would race though her mind as she rode the elevator up to her apartment, gazing at the buttons indicating the floors as they lit, hoping all the time that it would not stop for someone else to get on before it reaches her floor. She just didn't want to encounter any of her nosy neighbors, who would certainly try to delight her with their hypocrisies and insincere greetings.

All she wanted at the time and most other times was to get to her unit, her safe haven, away from the eyes and tongues of everyone, especially her neighbors. In her unit or haven, she could use her imagination to be whatever or whoever she wants to be.

Despite the falsehood, insensitivity, and hypocrisy toward her, uttered by her neighbors and others, there were a few people who knew her, who were more sensitive, honest and sincere in those dialogs or encounters with her. These individuals (myself included) would always try our best to sincerely convince her that with perseverance, she can achieve her goals and that she and all of us should heed the words of the song sung by the great reggae singer Jimmy Cliff, "You can get it if you really want, but you must try, try, try, and try, you'll succeed at last." We would also try to assure her that the true beauty of a genuinely good person is to be found within. Inner beauty is by far more important than physical attributes.

One day after carefully listening to the kind, sincere, and encouraging words of a couple who meant well, Irene turned to them and said, "I thank you for your encouraging words, but may I ask a question?"

"Certainly, please do," was their response.

Irene then asked, "If there are two candidates vying for the office of president of the United States of America, and one is not very smart, but very physically attractive, handsome, athletic, and charismatic, and the other is very smart, knowledgeable, but grossly overweight, obese, and definitely not physically attractive, which one would you vote for?"

MILTON

If there ever was a truly extraordinary person who everyone would like to meet, it would be Milton Berkowitz, an attorney turned mattress salesman, an amazingly knowledgeable, jolly, and spirited older guy, who was also a resident in this high-rise.

Milton or Uncle Milty never retired. He had always said retirement was not for him. "Why retire and sit around waiting to die?" He could often be heard saying, "I want to go down active," and "happy," he would add. He switched from being a lawyer to a salesman in his early sixties. He made the switch, he said, "Because being a lawyer he was surrounded by too much lies and deceptions," but he soon realized the world of sales was not much better; in fact, pretty much of the same was the order of the day.

Getting to know, or even just being around, him, for anyone, is like one of life's little treat. His humor, even though mostly dry or corny, would make even Oscar the grouch smile, simply by the way it was said, the expressions on his face while saying it, and his mannerisms. When lost in gloom, being in his presence will add some light to cheer you up, if even but a little.

Like many others, Milton liked to come to the lobby to talk with the doormen. Whenever he came when I am on duty, I considered it to be my treat for that day, and those days when he didn't show up left me wishing he would. Five minutes of Milty is all you need to get out of the blues and into a better mood. It's a gift he had that he himself was not even aware of.

Another talent that Milton possess is his extraordinary knowledge of geography, politics, and history. Name any country and he will tell you the capital city, how and in what year it became the capital. Not only can he name countries and capitals, he will also name the presidents, prime ministers, kings, queens, and dictators.

He knows the population count, the flags and their colors, and their national anthems. He is a living, breathing human geographical encyclopedia. And for a man who had never travelled outside the United States, all of this knowledge is truly amazing.

His knowledge extends beyond geography and politics. Milton also took a keen interest in music of the fifties, sixties, seventies, and eighties. If asked, he would accurately give the name of a song, the singer or singers, the writer, the year it debuted, and all other artists who did their renditions. Any song, any artist, any songwriter mentioned Milton will precisely identify, and when doing so without hesitation, searching, or stumbling for words. His vocabulary on these subjects is wholly admirable.

Because of his uncanny ability to learn and retain the things he knows, even though he is not a show-off, he is like a magnet for the many who gravitate toward him, whether to be entertained or to learn something from his pool of knowledge. We all like to engage in conversations with him, because at the end of the conversation, for what it's worth, we would leave with a joyful feeling and some added knowledge.

In his role as a mattress salesman, Milton often expressed to us that he had found his sense of purpose. He did not represent a store or a company. He was a one-man act; his sales route targeted the poorest of the boroughs of New York City where he went door to door and took orders for the most affordable mattresses. After taking the orders, he then goes to selected stores, mainly the smaller establishments and buy the merchandise paid from his own packet, then he would have these mattresses delivered to the families. After the deliveries are made, he goes to the addresses to ascertain that the families got their deliveries, and then he would make arrangements with them to pay a certain small amount each week until payment was made in full.

Milton had this idea long before it was adopted by the mainstream stores, and the introduction and emergence of the credit revolution and credit cards. And even after that, he kept on with his routes, helping people who could not qualify for credit or credit cards. Before Milton, these people, mostly newly arrived immigrants, from places like Central America, Eastern Europe, or the islands had layaway as their only option, as the system that remotely mimics credit.

Milton tried his hardest to help these people, because through his eyes, although very young then, he remembered the hardship his parents and grandparents endured when they arrived here from Poland. They had one used mattress handed down to them by other Poles who got here ahead of them and could eventually purchase a new one. Then they pass on the one that was handed down to them. These were tough times, and with only one mattress in the small two-room apartment, his parents had the children sleep on the mattress while they slept on the floor.

Although he sometimes made a small profit from his venture, and even though most of his customers were genuinely honest and needy, sometimes weeks would go by where they were just simply unable to make the payments. Milton would just let it slide and patiently wait until they were able to pay. There were some, when they saw him coming, they would hide because they were embarrassed for not having the money to pay him, embarrassed because they were fully aware that he was only doing his best to help out.

There were the few unscrupulous ones who he would often joke about whenever he told us of how they would hide from him, the excuses they came up with, and the various tactics they used when trying to avoid him.

There were also extreme cases where shortly after receiving the mattress, they would just disappear like a fart in the wind. But the dishonest ones didn't deter Milton from trying to help the others. His motto was, "After a long and hard day of work and being tested, a man needs to be rested."

At the front desk or round table, we are the first ones to see him as he emerges from his car when his wife drops him off at the front entrance, and after long hard days on the road, at his age, he sometimes barely stumbles in. We quietly say among ourselves, "What would we do without Milty?" Perhaps he owes his resiliency to his determination to help as many people as possible, coupled with the enjoyment and satisfaction he gets from making people laugh and the knowledge he imparts. After those long days on the road, we observed him dog-tired and limping through the lobby on his way to his apartment. Whatever the elixir is that he takes, perhaps we all need to take it.

The next day we would see a rejuvenated Milton, full of zest for someone of his age, telling jokes, sharing his knowledge of geography, music, and world affairs, at the same time asking us to give him erudite responses.

When it comes to being jolly, Santa Claus has nothing over Milton, but even as jolly as he was, he was ever aware of his mortality, more so due to his advanced years. During one-on-one conversations, he would reveal that if his wife of fifty years dies before him, he would wish to go also.

Then I would respond, asking, "Go where, Mr. Milton?"

And he would singingly respond, "Pushing up the daisies, pushing up the daisies!"

It is universally known that as we grow older, time seems to go faster, the years slips by quickly, and as time marches on, the words of my grandmother (even though she is long gone) continues to echo in my head or ears, "Once a man twice a child." She would often say, referring to the fact that if we get to see platinum years, we need to be nursed again, just as we needed to be nursed when we were babies or infants.

As the years slipped by for all of us, we watched with much concern and sadness the decline of Uncle Milty and his wife. Yet they continued with their daily sales run for as long as they could, until eventually and reluctantly (along with much prompting and persuading from their children), they gave it up.

Their decline progressed to the point where they both had to use walkers to get around, and unfortunately for us, we didn't get to see Milty as often as we were used to. In fact, we rarely saw him anymore.

One day, upon arriving at the high-rise or front desk to begin my shift, I was told by a colleague or fellow doorman that Uncle

Milton's children came and took both parents to a nursing home. Needless to say, his presence was greatly missed. His absence created a void in all whom he inspired, entertained, or came in contact with.

Several months later, we heard it through the grapevine that this wife had passed away six months after they were taken from their high-rise apartment. A year had passed and we did not know, nor wish to know the fate of Uncle Milty. We were aware that at his age and condition, it was highly unlikely that he would get better, but whether he was alive or dead, we wanted only to cement in our minds the fond, spirited, and inspired memories we have of him.

Throughout this journey we call life, we meet and encounter various persons with various personalities, ideologies, and outlooks. The impact that some of those individuals have or had on our lives, we become aware of immediately, realize much later or never at all, but if we are enlightened enough or possess the insight to banish the negative ideologies, embrace and learn from the positive, then pass these on to the people we meet along this journey, which in turn will be passed on to future generations, then this journey to death will, somehow, make sense.

Empty heads have long tongues.

—Kahlil Gibran

GASTON
(AKA MR. FALSE ONE,
AKA MR. BUDDINGTON)

In any place of work, any school, any neighborhood, any community, any village, or wherever one goes or whatever the situation in which one finds oneself, there will always be others among and around who will like or admire us, and surely, others who won't. It is one of those facts of life; how we handle the latter is primarily important.

Most of us humans do not like to be rejected, teased, or bullied; the ones who do not like us are usually the ones who will inflict these negatives on us. We in turn have to be aware of this fact of life, and not dwell on it, lest it will sink us into the swamp of depression. We need to learn how to, or not to engage these negative individuals who are likened to predators.

In the communities, schools, and neighborhoods, these individuals are always present, always waiting for, or to see someone to dislike for sometimes no apparent reason, or for ridiculous reasons fabricated in their small minds.

This high-rise has its fair share of these negative predators, some of whom are passive in their actions and others who are quite blatant. Of all the perpetually disgruntled people residing in this high-rise, there is one who stands out like a piece of spinach on a clean set of pearly whites.

This individual is an elderly male, whose face constantly displays the look of an angry gorilla. Unlike his fellow sourpuss counterparts who will dislike and complain about a handful of people, policies, rules, or things, he, on the other hand, either hates or disagrees with everyone and everything. In this case, we will refer to him as Mr. False One or Gaston.

Mr. False One has a complex. He not only thinks that everyone he comes across is out to get him, but also that every organization and every business is crooked. In this hi-rise building, he hates the condo board and its members; he constantly complains that they only became board members for the sole purpose of mismanaging and pocketing a portion of the maintenance fees, commonly known as common charges, paid in by the residents.

He is convinced that the board members and the management company are engaged in conspiracies to favor certain contractors and vendors who provide services to the building in order to receive monetary kickbacks to benefit themselves.

He opposes every building improvement plan put forward by the board. He harshly criticizes every project whether completed or in progress. He has negative comments on all the decorative aspects of the building's interior, from the light fixtures, the color of the walls, the plants, and down to the carpeting.

He makes permanent enemies of all who doesn't share and agree with his opinions or support his ideologies and rhetoric.

When it came to the employees, the superintendent, the doormen, and the porters, he spends major energy in disliking and discrediting us; in the case of the super, he swears that he sabotages the building's equipment and systems, such as the heating, cooling, and gas pipes. If a heating component in his apartment happened to fail for whatever reason, he would blame the super; wherein, if the super had sabotaged the heating system out of spite for him to not get heat, it would have affected all the other apartments above and below him, or for that matter, the entire building.

Mr. False One's hatred for the superintendent and the other members of the staff runs deep, with lies, deceptions, and false accusations. He has systematically tried to have all of us fired, one by one, with the doormen in particular. In the past, he would frequent the lobby or front desk to engage in conversations with us. We would only listen as he spewed out his words of disdain for the management company and the board. He would present himself at the lobby desk day after day, spending considerable time uttering the same negative things over and over

Usually, after the board and management get their share of bad mouthing, he would then begin bashing his neighbors and all others, whose opinions differ from his.

The extent of his deviousness sank to a new low when he made his visits to each doorman's shift and told each one to not trust the others, because he himself did not trust them either, thereby trying to create a rift among the staff members.

As for the various management companies who have managed this high-rise over the years, he hated every one of them and bombarded them with accusations of robbing the associations and residents of the buildings who hired them. According to him, they all were very good at cooking the books and does the same as the board does by favoring contractors who offered kickbacks.

He contends that all of these management companies are ineffective. In other words, "worthless," because rarely do they achieve the things that they were hired to do, which consists of maintaining the structural integrity of the building, keeping it spotless, doing necessary upgrades, and most important, keeping the common charges from skyrocketing; his contention is that they are all miserable failures.

He feels that if given the go ahead, he himself, along with a few likeminded individuals who ardently share his warped ideologies and support his opposition to the past and current operation of the building, would without question, do a better job of running the building than those incompetent outfits who call themselves property managers.

Without a doubt, Gaston is the least-liked person in this high-rise, judging from his words and actions, and how he has managed to alienate everyone he comes in contact with; almost all of the residents in the building think of him as stricken with or suffering from advanced paranoia, and that his actions are undoubtedly compulsive. They see no other way or reason how a person can be so extremely negative in his thoughts and actions and, in addition, so extremely angry.

If you happen to meet Gaston for the first time, even with a perpetually sour look on his face, coupled with his angry disposition, he possesses the ability to make you feel trusting and safe. When engaged in conversations with him, he will make you feel like a new-found friend, and that his anger and distrust is aimed at all others save the few, of which you would be one. Then in the short or long run, you will eventually feel the wrath of his twisted mind. He will turn against you as fast as the flip of a coin.

With some residents in the high-rise, he will fabricate lies and false accusations, and with others, he will stare piercingly at them in silence while displaying a look that could be described as sinister.

The ones who find themselves victims of his warped and paranoid state of mind should not try to rack their brains trying to figure out what they might have done or didn't do or said to offend him.

The truth or fact is, even an angel, a saint, or a person who would kiss his feet would be subjected to the same treatment. It reached a point where everyone in the building steers clear of him and goes out of their way to avoid him. If they are about to get on the elevator and when the door opens he is in it, they will step back and not get on, or if they are in it and the door opens and they see him there about to get on board they would get off, even if it is not the floor they intended, they would rather take the stairs the rest of the way.

I would imagine that there are many Gaston False Ones in our midst, our buildings, our high-rises, our neighborhoods, our towns, our cities, and in societies all over the world—angry and paranoid souls, who unknowingly need help, psychological and emotional, help that would hopefully help to enlighten them to the realization that although this life, this existence is filled with adversities, disappointments, and gloom, there still exists some degree of beauty and simplicity in people and in nature, which makes life meaningful and worth living.

We may ponder, what is wrong in our societies that breads angry people like Gaston? Aren't these angry, hateful, devious and violent individuals just like the rest of us? Who not so long ago peed and pooped on ourselves, when all we could do was cry and our mothers would have to clean us up, and wash, wipe, and powder our stinky little bottoms, then cuddle, pamper, and cradle us in the warmth of their bosoms, giving us their unconditional love.

There are those among us who struggle to find answers for the ills in our societies and dream of a utopian brotherhood, which possibly may be unattainable, due to religion, greed, so-called race, class, and social inequalities to name a few. These may be the factors which produce individuals like Gaston False One.

Maybe someday, a Zeitgeist of enlightenment will come upon us, a time when lies, falsehood, and sarcasm are rejected by all of us, a time when peace, love, and brotherhood becomes the norm, a time when we realize that we are all sitting in the same life boat, which is being rocked and tossed about by life's stormy seas.

Until that utopian day arrives, we will remain stuck with all the Gaston False Ones and others who are even worse. For those who encounter or interact with these individuals, in order to maintain sanity and to avoid being stressed and depressed from the negative energy that surrounds them like halos. We need to fortify our minds and be thick-skinned, like our politicians who, when negative criticisms, insults, and blames are thrown at them, these things will just simply bounce off their hides as they walk away with their "don't give a damn" attitudes.

MRS. WILBERG

For those of us who thinks that growing old is crappy, those who are downright scared of this reality, and people like Heinrich who refers to himself and others who are as old as he is as "old fucks" an expression he said is commonly used in Germany when referring to old folks, all need to adopt a page from the book of Etta Wilberg.

Compared to the other older people living in this high-rise, Etta, even though being a lot older than they are, is a relative newcomer to the building, where others have lived here for over a quarter of a century. She, along with her husband, moved into their unit about ten years ago, then approximately six and a half to seven years after moving in her husband, who was a few years younger than her, died.

In many cases, when two people have been together for more than five decades, when one dies, the surviving half is usually so torn apart and so bewildered that they also die shortly after, but not so with Etta. Surely, she mourned the death of her husband, but she also took it with a deep understanding of inevitability. When asked how she is coping, her answer would be, "I am trying my best, but I must say that Norris and I had a good and a long life together, and I am holding onto and cherishing those precious memories."

Now at one hundred and three years young, she is an inspiration to everyone young and old in this high-rise and wherever she goes. She inspires us by way of her positive attitude and outlook on life and her encouragingly positive ways, advices, and encouragements.

At her advanced age, she has managed to reignite and rejuvenate the long-lost energy in the older population in this high-rise; she is like an oasis in a desert of old sand. Most of the encounters, interactions, and conversations between her and others take place in the lobby, where she often sits while awaiting the arrival of her daughter, who often picks her up to take her out for lunches, dinners, shopping, or visiting others.

Amazingly, she remembers everyone by name, and whenever she sits waiting, she would beckon to us to come over, but even without her beckoning to us, at all times when we see her, we would instinctively gravitate toward her, like young ones staying close to their mothers. We always sit with her, holding her hands as she talks to us with words and statements so positive, so uplifting, and so welcoming, especially for us, the doorman, who are the recorders of complains and the takers of blames.

On any given day, after listening to some residents who are irate, expressing their disgruntled grouses, her encouraging words are like elixir from the gods. Likewise, if we get her words of encouragements, before listening to the problems, complaints, and displeasures, it fortifies us with an armor of strength to get us through the day.

Her words, expressions, and statements are very simple, yet powerful in their simplicity, listening to her is like hearing echoes of my grandmother, who was always teaching us (her grandchildren) about the complexities, the joys, the expectations, and the disappointments we should expect in life. I can clearly recall the quotations she used when teaching us about good manners and courtesy, and also when she would scold us for misbehaving.

Some of the quotations she used were from books she read. Some she memorized from times passed, when her own grandmother would teach or scold her, and others written in her mind, results of her own life experiences and cards dealt to her by whomever or whatever the dealer was.

Whenever we misbehave or disobeyed her, she would say, "My child, your continued disobedience and misbehavior may go on for long, but it won't be forever." Or the times when we were being lazy, she would say, "Remember now, the lazy birds makes smaller droppings," which at that time to us sounded like complete nonsense. The latter, for example, meant the birds who puts the time and effort and worked to catch the worms would surely fill their stomachs, but the ones who sat around chirping and puts very little effort into going after and catching the worms would end up with very little or nothing in their stomachs; therefore, they will be so hungry that when they poop, it would be tiny bits. The moral, determination along with hard work pays off.

It is such a great pity that as children, our brains are so underdeveloped and our consciousness so unaware that all of the wisdom and logic imbedded in the guidance and counseling which she inexhaustibly tried to instill in us, by way of her quotations and stories, we just couldn't see, it was later when she was gone, and during times of solitude or gatherings, when we remember and reflect on the things she said to us, we can't help but think, "why it took that long for us to fully comprehend her reason. Now in adulthood, we are filled with regret that we did not take her words with more humility, which brings me back to Mrs. Wilberg.

Whenever Mrs. Wilberg came to the lobby, she would immediately acknowledge whoever is on duty at the front desk with a warm greeting, and as she sat awaiting the arrival of her daughter, she would begin telling of her life's journey.

Being a woman of Jewish heritage, she spoke of the barriers, obstacles, and hurdles she encountered along the way, the doubters, and naysayers who said and did everything they could to discourage her and Norris when they embarked on their first business venture, which eventually turned out to be an overwhelming success due to hard work, positive thinking, and perseverance.

Like my grandmother, she spoke of the many fears that we all need to overcome in our journeys. She would often emphasize the roles her grandparents played in her development into adulthood. They were bastions of honesty and values that they imparted in their own creative ways.

Although, by nature, she's an optimist, Etta is fully aware that there is a negative to the process of life, and with this in mind (like my grandmother), she spoke clearly about the obstacles, hurdles, and snares we will face in our lives; but being the person she is, after speaking about the negatives, she would immediately follow up with suggestions of ways or actions we can take to get by and what she did to keep up and how she conquered those negatives.

We are all aware that at her age of one hundred and three, most of us will never attain, therefore, when she speaks, we listen, and listen we do, because even at that age, her clarity is simply astounding.

Her advices may sound simple, yet very effective. Her voice, though soft and calm, echoes through my mind when she said, "Whatever is bothering you now, or whoever is making you upset, be strong and try to outlast it or them, and eventually, it will pass. It always does."

When she counseled us on work, "Work hard," she said, "but don't overdo it. Listen and take heed to the dictates of your body. Just remember that everything has a breaking point, and some things, when they break, are irreparable. Know when to take a break. Go on vacations as often as possible, but don't put yourself in debt to do so. Save toward it. Don't charge it. Put some pennies away especially for the occasion. Pennies becomes dollars, and furthermore, being in and worrying about debt could send you to an early grave.

As she got a bit more comfortable, easing back in her chair, she continued, "I cannot begin to tell you the scores of people who have asked me, what is the secret or secrets of my longevity and sharpness of mind at my age. Whenever this question is asked of me, I can only smile, because I truly don't know the answer or answers, and I also don't know if there are any, luck perhaps, but there are a few things which I think could have benefited me greatly, and I will share them with you." At that point she began.

"Balance, live a balanced life. As I have always said, too much of anything, even positive things, if overdone, could end up being negative or detrimental to one's well-being.

"Greed—try your best to overcome greed. It is one of the worst word in any language. It will poison your mind, and when that happens, it can become contagious and infect even those among us with the purest intentions. Once infected, selfishness sets in, which results in rejection, isolation, and unhappiness. A perfect example could be found in Mr. Scrooge.

"Forgive, oh yes! Forgiving, we must all learn to forgive. It is a great and miraculous healer. Forgiving heals us not only spiritually but also physically. In order to live a life of peace and contentment, and to be truly happy, we must let go of our angers and unnecessary fears. We must learn to forgive even those who have done us wrong, and even if those we forgive are unaware of our forgivingness, by forgiving, we will at least find peace within ourselves. Anger is an invisible foe, which robs us of the complete enjoyment of life and renders us miserable and uncomfortable, not only with ourselves, but also for others who finds it necessary to engage us. We should show kindness to our fellow humans. All people, no matter where they are from, how they look, or their social status, they are our brothers and sisters. Our kindness should also be extended to all humble living things.

"Friendship, very important, my child. You've heard the phrase 'no man is an island.' Well, it is true. The human animal, other species of animals, and all living things are all connected to each other and to the source that gives energy to all things.

"Imagine yourself being the only person left on planet Earth after a catastrophe that killed everyone else. With no one to interact with, isolation, boredom, and insanity will take hold, and believe it or not, loneliness and isolation will shorten your days; it is for this reason that one of the most severe form of punishment for prisoners is solitary confinement.

"Not all of us are good; unfortunately, some of us have adopted selfish, devious, and conniving ways, a direct contrast to those among us with good attributes. Throughout your life, you will, as I have, cross paths with monsters, vampires, saints, and angels, and as my grandfather would say, 'If you lie down with dirty dogs, you will rise with flees,' so, my child, choose your friends wisely, and with so doing, you will have them for life."

"Finding genuine friendship is like finding the mother lode in an abandoned mine, knowing that someone or others are ready to stand with you and to offer advice, support, or consolation at times when necessary. And for them to know that if the table is turned, it would undoubtedly be a mutual response."

"Family," Etta continued, "a family in harmony is unbreakable. Their underlying strength is as solid as the rock of Gibraltar. When in unison, family members share a common bond that runs deeper than them being the best of friends. It forms the core of their union, and they will almost always offer a depth of support that goes beyond what your circle of genuine friends can ever offer."

"This type of bond is not merely an emotional one; it is an innate, inescapable process, much like little chicks or ducklings will cling to their mothers and find safe haven under their mother wings. My child, it is a blood bond. The love and support shown to me by my family has carried me through times of doubt and uncertainties and have, in many ways, contributed to my emotional and physical well-being, as well as my longevity."

"My diet is also the subject of many a questions, judging from the number of times I have been asked 'to what foods do you owe your amazingly good health and longevity and what foods do you avoid?" Please tell us about your diet.' I am sure that the people who ask are those who wish to have a long and healthy journey in this life."

"For each person who ask, my answer has always been the same, 'I don't follow any special diet. I eat anything that I like, but I try to not fill my stomach to its capacity. I enjoy most of the same foods that you all eat and have been eating since childhood, but if I must give some form of credit to one type of food in particular, it would be beans. I eat lots of it."

"Beans seem to have contributed to my good health." She chuckled as she added, "Sure, it makes me very flatulent, but for the sake of its health benefits, Norris and I had learned to tolerate that aspect of it." Upon hearing her take on beans and her closing statement on it, we all chuckled along with her.

She kept on smiling as she slowly turned her head, scanning our faces as we smiled in admiration of her humor, then she said, "It lifts my spirits and makes me very happy to be surrounded by smiling faces. Having a good sense of humor and to have a humorous style are vital ingredients for health and longevity, and laughter is a potent elixir for the mind, body, and spirit. And, my child, never forget the three Ls—laugh, love, and live."

Of all the things this little old has said to us, there is one which, for all that it's worth, has stuck with me and made a lasting imprint on my mind. On one of her memorable visits to the lobby, after her usual encouraging thoughts and inspiring words and statements, her daughter had just pulled her car up to the front entrance; as she stood up and walked toward the door, she paused and said, "We humans create various ways to make life complicated, but the secret to a beautiful life lies within its simplicity."

"Remember also, that in life there will be things and even people you truly like or love, wherein a time may come when you have to give the things up, and let go of the people in order to move forward."

THE PORTERS
(EDWARDO)

Porters are vital components in any building; they work hard to keep the buildings clean, which is their primary duty. But like the doormen, they are called upon to do or assist with various non-job description activities.

The porters and doormen are, in most cases, bosom buddies. For one, they are quite aware that they are at the very bottom of the socio-economic ladder, and that some of the residents and their guests view them as bums or dumb asses who either lack ambition or just simply could not make it academically.

I cannot speak of other buildings, but in this high-rise, almost all the porters who worked here in the past and the present ones are from Central America, and after talking to and getting to know them, one will find that these are smart and colorful individuals with interesting pasts and backgrounds, and that in their home countries, they held jobs with higher positions and were respected in their social circles.

The chief reason for most of them being here in this country is the almighty dollar. The greenback is perpetually so strong against their currency that despite being well-educated and with good positions, the money they made did not go far. They, therefore, found it very hard to make ends meet. The magnetic lure of the dollar becomes so irresistible that they reluctantly leave their families behind to venture into lands unknown to them, all prepared for working as hard as they can, with their minds set on sending most of what they will earn back home so that their families can live more comfortably.

Eduardo made his sacrificial journey twenty-seven years ago and has been a porter in this high-rise for the past twenty-five years. A short, mild-mannered man with a pleasant countenance and a contagious smile, he left us captivated when he told the story of his journey to the United States of America.

He spoke of the long, hot days and cold nights walking through and across the Mexican badlands and deserts while being constantly on the lookout, with the awareness that there were armed "banditos" who prey upon stragglers like himself, to rob them of their last penny or even kill them for no particular reason. He told us of how he quickly learned that survival throughout that harrowing journey meant banding together with other stragglers to form a group in order to look out for each other.

His small group got to a point where they were intercepted by smugglers who convinced them that they could get them safely across the border at a cost. The cost would be whatever money or valuables they had in their packets or bags at that time plus a certain amount to be paid in cash after getting them over the border.

He described how they were taken across, crammed like canned sardines in a small, specially built, hidden compartment in the back of a box truck, with only a few cleverly concealed tiny holes to allow some air in so that they could at least breathe. "We were sweating like pigs. There was so much perspiration. It felt like we were laying in shallow water."

"After crossing the border, we were held in a locked room just slightly larger than a jail cell, where we slept on the bare floor. We were not allowed any contact with anyone. We had to give them the contact information for our families back home, or for relatives we had in the United States. In doing so, they would make contact with our relatives to demand payment."

"It was near the end of the third week when they allowed a few of us to leave, the ones who they received some form of payment from the families or relatives. The whole ordeal was so punishing that I could not help feeling sorry for myself, but I felt even sorrier for the others who were still locked in that steamy, smelly room."

"After a month of not taking a shower, you could only imagine the odor coming from the bodies in that room, both men and women. To this day, I kept on wondering what became of the others. There were some families I personally knew who had nothing of any value and no money. Hopefully, the ones I said goodbye to in the room that day are still alive. Today, I can still see the look of fear on their faces as I stumbled out."

"My journey continued when I boarded a train in Texas and ended when I disembarked in Connecticut." He was met at the train station by a friend of one of his cousins back home. This kind person who had arranged his train trip also accommodated him with free room and board until he could get on his own two feet. He was willing to help out, because he remembered a similar journey he made eighteen years ago.

Faced with a new environment, a different way of thinking, a totally faster-paced society than which he was familiar with and not a word of English, Eduardo knew what he had to do. He quickly signed up with a locally ran program teaching English as a second language to immigrants, and with his eagerness, he learned quickly. He picked up a few odd jobs here and there, then he heard about a United States government amnesty program, which he applied for. Sometime after he got a work permit and through word-of-mouth connections, he landed the fateful job as a porter in this high-rise building.

This position as porter has consumed him and became somewhat of a new career. He became one of the most dedicated porters the residents have ever had. He was hard working and very well liked by most of them. He worked closely with the superintendent and learned from him a lot about the mechanics of the building. After his regular shift ends, he could be found in any of a number of apartments in the high-rise, helping the residents with tasks, like window washing, waxing floors, cleaning air-conditioning filters, organizing and dumping stuff, and a host of other odd jobs.

Not only did the residents liked the convenience of having someone at their beck and call, but in doing those extra jobs, he was able to send more money back home to his family. From doing these jobs, he got to know very well the habits of some of the people. He once told me with a smile on his face, that from helping them with organizing and dumping, he saw who had the biggest stash of girlie magazines and X-rated videos and which ladies had under their beds the biggest box of vibrating toys. He did not say who these people were, and I did not ask.

Despite being a generally jovial person, in a pensive mood, he once reveled to me that in retrospect, he is not sure that the sacrifice he made was the best decision, because he missed out on the childhood of his children who he dearly loves, and even though they are now grown and understand and appreciate the sacrifice he made for them, which deepened their love for him even more, but even with the knowledge of their love, admiration, and understanding, he admits to, at times, asking himself, "Was it worth it?"

JAVIER

"Guatemaltecos" is the word that the Guatemalan men use jokingly to describe their nationality. "Chimador" is the word used by them to describe men who are over virile, over macho, and over horny. These descriptions aptly describe Javier, a porter who has worked in this high-rise for the better part of seventeen years.

There was nothing special or outstanding about Javier. He was not a sharp dresser. He was not at all muscular. He was short with a distinct paunch and an accent so heavy that after every statement he made, he had to be asked, "Can you repeat that, please" from which he often got annoyed from us asking him to always repeat what he said. He was certainly not rich; hence his position as a porter, but despite all of his shortcomings, if there is one thing in which he was not lacking, it's confidence.

He gave the impression that, with a little effort and charm, he could get and bed any woman he chose to go after. He could go on for hours bragging about the many women he had had over the years. We often had to stop him from getting into the details of his activities.

With his seemingly insatiable carnal attitude, he was smart enough to not go after any of the residents in this high-rise building, but that didn't stop him from fantasizing about the ones he thought were desirable in his eyes; whenever we would muster in the break room, he would begin to tell us how and what he would do if he got together with any of the ones he liked.

It is quite typical for us as men, when we gather socially, to talk about the type of women we like, but Javier was always too extreme for us, and when he went too far, we would immediately change the subject, then he would get the message and shut up.

Although being a man in his fifties, he considered any woman over the age of twenty-five to be too old for him. He explained that he was following a tradition in his country where women over twenty-five thinks of themselves as being too old. With this in mind, he made frequent visits to Guatemala, in pursuit of those misguided women.

Javier had convinced himself that what his wife of twenty-two years didn't know wouldn't hurt her; therefore, he went on with his carnal meanderings and gave himself a license to continue on, and that he did.

When in the lobby mopping the floor or washing the windows, he kept a keen eye on the street, always on the lookout for the ladies passing by, and each time he spotted one, he would gaze at their rear ends, and the ones he thought were exceptionally enticing, he would go nuts over, by turning to us, saying, "Wow, look at that. Did you see that?" Sometimes we would take a look, but we mostly ignore him or say "yeah, yeah, yeah."

In the middle of one of his daily lustful conversations, I interrupted, saying, "Javier, may I ask you a question?" He said sure with a hint of annoyance, as if to say, why did you interrupt me in the middle of a juicy story?

"Do you love your wife?" I asked.

"Yes, indeed," he answered.

"And does your wife love you?" I continued.

"Absolutely," he replied.

"Splendid," I replied. "Now I will tell you a true story about someone I know."

"Okay," he said, "but make it short, so that I can finish mine."

"Lester is a guy with the same disposition as you. He has a carnal mind. He just cannot resist the temptations of the flesh, and he is a womanizer. He had a lovely wife whom he swore loved him. One evening, he stopped at a bar to have a beer with a friend. He couldn't keep his eyes off a lady sitting at the other end of the bar. He said to himself, 'Damn it, I'll go over and introduce myself,' so he went over, and after a few minutes they were smiling and giggling with each other. His friend, now totally ignored, got fed up and left.

"Lester was so engrossed with the woman that he did not even notice that his friend had left. As the evening wore on, Lester and the woman were now leaning on each other. Things became so heated that they decided to finish it off at a motel at the other side of town.

"They arrived at the motel, and after checking in, they walked across the lobby toward the elevator, still leaning against and making spontaneous kisses on the lips both to each other. As they approached the elevator, the door opened and out stepped his wife on the arm of another man, leaning against and kissing each other after a seemingly satisfying session in the room they were in. So there they were, him checking in with his lady friend, and she checking out with a lover.

"Lester's face went pale. The impact of the encounter was so overwhelming that he felt as if he was about to shit his pants. Both he and his wife were locked in a prolonged stare, he with anger and surprise in his eyes, and she with surprise and revenge in hers. He was surprised to find his wife cheating on him. She was surprised that fate had brought them to the same motel, but felt revenged, because, all along, she knew of his infidelity but until now, had chosen to remain passive about it.

"So, Javier," I continued, "put yourself in Lester's place or position. Now tell me, how would you have felt and what would you have done?"

Without even a second thought, Javier exclaimed, "Divorce!"

"But why?" asked the other porter who was nearby and had been listening to Javier boasting about his prowess in bed. "How is it that you can and your wife can't? Wouldn't you just be getting a dose of your own medicine?'

He responded, "Men can, but women shouldn't be doing that sort of thing."

At that very moment, we realized that he was caught in the grips of ignorance and denial, or could it be just plain stupidity?

BIG CAL

Here in this high-rise, we had a superintendent who was a classic Harley man, a biker in the true sense of the term. Cal Rider, a.k.a. Big Cal, the brawny type with big hands similar to a bear's paw, his deep raspy voice resonated with power and authority. He grasped and moved things around with such little effort, one would think he had the strength of a grizzly.

With just a glimpse of his size, he is the type that would make you say, "Boy, that is one guy I would not like to get into a fight with" or "In a brawl, he is one guy I would like to have on my side."

Big Cal, as he was called by everyone, gets really angry if you mess with or talk bad about the two things he felt passionate about, his family and his 1965 (classic) Harley Davidson motorcycle, and one look at him when he's angry would make anyone want to turn and go the other way. In an angry mood, his eyes would bulge like a frog.

Each morning before the start of work, we would all gather (porters, doormen, and the super) for coffee or tea, and during those times, when we talked, joked, and laughed about the trivialities of life and work, Big Cal's voice roared above all, and whenever a point was made that he found to be either amusing, serious, or ridiculous, his voice would tower and echo, with his favorite phrase, which was "what the fuck."

Despite his size, intimidating appearance, and in-your-face, tell-it-like-it-is attitude, he showed respect for others. His motto was, "Don't fuck with me, and I won't fuck with you."

He had been the superintendent of the building for over thirty years. All that time spent, he said, working in the high-rise had made him a humbler person, and it might have saved his life. He had just been initiated in a notorious motorcycle gang when he got the job as superintendent of this high-rise. The responsibilities of maintaining the building offered him very little time to ride with the group. Eventually, he broke from the group, then little by little, he learned that most of its members were deceased. Some died in accidents involving their motorcycles, some from violent clashes with rival bikers, and others were thrown in the slammer for fighting and brawls that left others seriously injured.

Over the years, he had acquired a significant and vast amount of knowledge in building repairs and maintenance, skills and knowledge that he gladly imparted to any or all the porters and doormen, if they were willing to learn.

Old habits die hard, so although heavily burdened with the building's never-ending work load, he made Friday evenings his time to pull his old Harley out for a quick ride. Accompanied by an old buddy of his who was also a super in a nearby high-rise, and like Cal, a diehard Harley man, after a quick ride and with the motorcycles back in their garage spaces, Big Cal and his buddy would wander off on foot toward the local bars, and in the wee hours of the night, after the bartender's last call, they could be seen stumbling home (every Friday night or Saturday morning like clockwork) as drunk as skunks.

Unlike Big Cal who is quick-tempered and does not hold anything back, if he thinks that you are an ass, he will (without hesitation) tell you to your face, Cal's wife was a quiet woman with beautiful features shadowed by her sad eyes. For them, finding each other proved that opposites can and does attract.

We would never have imagined a rough and tough swashbuckling type like Big Cal settling down with a quiet, humble, calm, and modest woman. As humble as she was, their three children—a daughter and two sons—flocked more to her for advice and guidance. She did a good job of keeping her daughter away from the boys with only one thing in their minds and her son away from the wrong influences, and she was a good mother and a calming influence on Big Cal.

We all have our own faults and weaknesses, hers was tobacco. She mostly did not smoke in the presence of her children. In times of indulgence, she took to the far side of the building, and at nights, when they were fast asleep, she would pace the sidewalk at the front of the building, smoking while gathering her thoughts.

In life, reactions often follow actions. After bouts of continuous coughing got worse, Cal's wife was diagnosed with lung cancer. During the first several months, it seemed as if she was winning her fight against the disease, but suddenly, she took a turn for the worse and deteriorated rapidly. This beautiful, humble soul eventually paid her ultimate price for her weakness. The day she died we had never before seen a grown man cry to the extent that Cal did. Big Cal didn't just cry—he hollered, he bawled, he wailed, he wept.

Just like the bouts of coughing his wife had, he had bouts of crying, mixed with despair, disbelief, and anger. It seemed that he would never again be the same. This brawny, tough-as-nails man was now a baby again. With the emotional turmoil he was going through, he became somewhat reclusive.

After reluctantly working each day, he would quietly retreat to his quarters to be with his children who were also deeply saddened and shaken by the loss of their beloved mother.

Of all the pent-up emotions in his head, anger was the one mostly felt and expressed by Cal. He was angry with himself and with God, angry because he felt as if he did not do all the things he could, and should have done for her. Words that remained unsaid that should have been said left him with a feeling of guilt that perhaps only time can erase.

He was angry with God for taking this humble person so soon when the world is full of evil sons of bitches that should be taken out or struck with diseases. "And I know quite a number of them," he said, yet they are still around enjoying the bad things they do to others and enjoying their lives.

As the years went by, his anger dissipated a little. His two older children moved out, which he knew would eventually happen, but still made him feel more alone. As he got older, he could feel his own health slipping away, but showed no interest in getting himself checked. One evening, while sitting alone in his apartment reminiscing about his life and the time he spent as a soldier in Vietnam and how that experience had affected him in many ways, his old Harley buddy unexpectedly stopped by for a quick visit. During that visit, his friend convinced him that they should dust off their Harleys and start riding again regularly.

Within a short period of time, they were out riding two to three evenings a week. Weekends would find them polishing their bikes, then going for long-distance rides. They met up with other like-minded old-timers who had also dusted off their Harley Davidsons. They formed their own gang and rediscovered a freedom they had long lost—the wind swishing at their collars, the open roads, the horizon in the distance, and a feeling of oneness with a finely tuned machine. To a biker, this is the ultimate freedom.

Although not feeling in the best of health, for the first time since his wife died, we saw Big Cal smiling again. As the months slipped by, his health was also slipping; he rode with the gang, sometimes alone or with his old buddy as often as he could.

As his health waned, he would sometimes drag himself out and onto his motorcycle for another ride, another taste of freedom. His refusal to get medical attention came to an end when, one day while attempting to mount his bike, it toppled over with him. He was taken to the hospital where he was treated and sent home. A few weeks later he was diagnosed with bladder cancer.

After he became aware of his diagnosis, his condition took a turn for the worse. Deterioration came rapidly. Unable to control his bladder, he was fitted with a permanent bag. We watched as this mountain of a man, proud and strong, reduced to frailty and frequent bed-wetting accidents. He became a shell of what he once was. His inability to perform his duties left Eduardo doubling down to pick up the slack.

In his heyday, his presence was so powerful that when he entered a room or wherever he went, others would move aside to make room for him, similar to a great white shark, where the other sea creatures would get out of its way when it's coming through. Remembering his past stature and the powerful effect he had on others, he did not want to be seen in his present condition, so he quietly retreated to a remote location in Maine, where he had a few close friends who understood his plight and were willing to help in whichever way they could.

The only people who he allowed to visit him were his children and his biker buddies. His main biker buddy who visited him frequently while he was still superintendent at the high-rise kept us informed on Big Cal's condition.

It is said that a person in their deathbed, conscious of the realization that the end is near, may have flashbacks of events experienced through their life's journey. If they had secrets that were never before divulged, those secrets may be spilled out at that time.

Cal's biker buddy told us that, nearing the end, Cal spoke feebly but continuously. He continued saying that the words Cal uttered made him more conscious of himself, his goals, his purpose, how he relates to others, and his own mortality. The things expressed by Cal, he said, all or most of us could somehow relate to. He regretted not taking the time and effort to do all the things he had always wanted to do but kept putting off for later, which never came, regretted not being more affectionate with his wife, which, upon her passing, left him with the feeling of utter guilt, regretted not being more flexible and accepting of other people and cultures, angry with himself for being a lifelong procrastinator and pussyfooter hiding behind a tough-guy facade, all the time trying to be another Leroy Brown.

MRS. VAN GELBAND

Apart from the sourpusses, adult spoilt brats, and blamers, there are some genuinely classy and sophisticated individuals residing in this high-rise. Above all, Mrs. Gelband is the most outstanding. She epitomizes style, charisma, and class. She is sophistication personified, a real woman of substance— well-spoken, well-travelled, cultured, and worldly.

Her position as assistant to an ambassador gave her exposure to many countries, peoples, and cultures. This exposure has made her a well-balanced person, and even with her level of aristocracy, she never failed to acknowledge and engage us (the doormen) in conversations.

I can recall the beginning of my employment at the high-rise; it was during the second week stationed at the front desk when I first saw Mrs. Van Gelband. With my face down, I was in the process of writing a work order, I heard the sound of a car braking. I looked up and saw a limousine pull up at the front of the building, and out stepped Mrs. Van Gelband and a small entourage. She had just returned from a weeklong series of meetings in Europe. I remember uttering quietly, "Wow, who is this lady?"

Along with her two matrons, they entered the lobby. There were so many suitcases it made me wonder how the airline allowed it, and the entire scene seemingly pulsated with glitz, glamour, and regality. Her two assistants wore shimmering sequin-type dresses, and Mrs. Gelband wore a red carpet-style dress with an attached piece that looked like Lord Vader's cape, and as they breezed through the lobby, the cape gently lifted away from her body as it mingled with the backwind, and as we felt the energy of their presence, it felt as if Vader had switched to the good side of the force and was passing through.

As the time passed, our polite and brief greetings became short conversations, which turned into longer ones. Most of those short conversations happened at the lobby desk or round table while she awaited limousine service, which took her to the Metropolitan Opera. The lengthier conversations happened on my off-duty times when I voluntarily drove her to medical appointments, and in those more private, away-from-the-desk, relaxed times she spoke of her life before she came to this high-rise.

Her husband, before he died, was a successful businessman and dealmaker, who traveled extensively nationally and internationally and was also charming, flirtatious, and charismatic. Together, they bought and lived in a mansion in a nearby affluent, upscale upper-upper community, a zip code where only the one-percenters can afford to live.

They attended many "five and up to twenty thousand dollars a plate" events and donated large sums of monies to politicians whose policies they agreed with. Their circle of friends and neighbors were all well-heeled, well-traveled, drank the most expensive wines, ate the richest foods, wore designer clothes, drove expensive cars. They've been there, done that.

At their regular house parties (each time held and hosted randomly at a different house within their wide circle), they would in little groups chitchat and boast about their stocks and investment portfolios, their real estate holdings, their wardrobes, their automobiles, their country club affiliations, and so on. Mrs. Van Gelband explained that living that type of lifestyle offered all the material privileges in our society, but on a broad scale, in her mind, there was a great degree of superficiality in living to compete with the Joneses.

In her broad circle, she could not recall anyone boasting about their charitable donations, because including herself, they gave nothing to charity, but there was no lack of announcing and boasting of the huge donations to would-be mayors, governors, senators, and the like.

There were many things she observed within her circle of friends that convinced her that she had to make an exit, most of them passively competing to see who has the most, the biggest, the most expansive, or the most elaborate, and the hypocrisy and gossiping that came hand in hand with the silent competition. But her exit came even faster than she had planned due to the ever-increasing practice of wife- or husband-swapping within her circle. She had seen and heard actions and words that gave her subtle hints of those hedonistic activities and encounters.

It finely became quite clear on one of their ladies' luncheon at a country club, while sitting in a group of six ladies, chatting about the hot summer weather, politics, foods, and their husbands. She was taken aback when one of the ladies said, "Well, my dear, my Harold has been dreaming about you. Would you and Arnie like to join us after the party this Friday night?" She momentarily froze from not knowing how to respond, then she glanced of the faces of the other women to see what their expressions would be, but to her surprise, they just continued chatting away about their husbands. Knowing quite well what joining them meant and at the same time not knowing exactly how to respond, she paused for a moment, then in a mild, somewhat sarcastic tone quickly replied, "Oh, how thoughtful of you, but my Arnie hasn't been feeling well of late; therefore, we must decline."

When she told her husband about what had transpired, little did she know that she was in for an even-bigger surprise when Arnie revealed that he knew about the activities and, in fact, wanted to participate but was afraid to approach her with it. It was then that she became aware of the pervasiveness of this practice within their circle of friends and, apparently, of other couples and groups outside of their circle but within their community who are joining in on the fun and action. Her summary of the happenings is that with this privileged and materially successful lifestyle, these people have experienced everything that money can buy. They've tried almost everything, from pot and cocaine to running with the bulls, and many have even gone hunting in Zimbabwe, killing the innocent animals for the sake of hanging their heads as trophies on the walls of their stately mansions.

It got to the point where she just couldn't take that lifestyle anymore, and then one night after retiring for the evening, as they lay half asleep in the darkness of their bed chamber, suddenly her voice jolted Arnie out of his dozed state, as it sliced the darkness in the room, like an invisible knife. "Arnold, we must sell this place and get away from here," she said.

At first he resisted, for the mere fact that he didn't mind the intimate get-togethers and was actually hoping to get involved, but when his health took a downturn, naturally his libido, along with his curiosity, waned. Two months before their house finally sold, he succumbed to his illness.

The lifestyle that she came to dislike so much, for so many reasons, was now a thing of the past, and is now faded memories, but even though her Arnie was in favor of that type of lifestyle and liked all that came along with it (including the extra activities), her love for him never faded She mourned his death deeply.

With the understanding that the lifestyle she gave up is filled with the things most of us crave and dream of, she now lives in a modest apartment, enjoys her job as the assistant to an ambassador, which opened her mind to the world of plain and ordinary folks, rich in their own simple ways and cultures; she explained that the fancy dresses are only special occasions, and in her position, she had the choice of hiring one or two assistants, so she picked and hired two likeminded widows who also wanted to see the world from a different perspective, and with open minds.

With her position and job description, she had to still mingle with the elites and elite wannabes but with a completely different mind-set. She now describes her mission and purpose as messenger of the so-called common people, the disadvantaged, the downtrodden, the underdogs, the forgotten, and the unsung heroes.

For those among us who not only dream of being wealthy but are actively engaged in plans, projects, and schemes, with goals set to achieve fortune and fame, she wishes luck and success, but with words of advice and caution: "When you've achieved your goals, be aware and beware of the double-headed monster who, if allowed, will take control of your mind, your thoughts, and your soul and will eventually consume you. This monster's heads are selfishness and greed.

If you can't fly, then run
If you can't run, then walk
If you can't walk, then crawl
But whatever you do, you have
To keep moving forward.

—Martin Luther King Jr.

SMILEY

His is a face not easily forgotten. His smile just the same, and what a guy behind both. He had to be the happiest person in this high-rise and, perhaps, the whole neighborhood. Humphrey has a permanent smile on his face, reminiscent of the Mona Lisa. The only difference is, his smile displays his pearly whites.

Whenever he approaches, whether from near or from a distance, his teeth always lead the way. His smile does not go away even when he speaks, which makes it very contagious. In the past, whenever he came to the front desk, I had to sometimes ask myself, "Am I smiling in accord with him, or am I smiling at the fact that he is always smiling?" And if I found that I was smiling in disbelief of his constant smile and not smiling along with him, I would rebuke myself, because in the world we live in today, with all its misery and mayhem, to meet a person who is always smiling is truly uplifting and gives us a feeling of hope.

Humphrey's ambitions and aspirations are just as constant as his joviality. He lives a life of make- believe in his own make-believe world and has a certain fascination with the corporate world. Although unemployed, he gets up early each morning and puts on a suit and shiny dress shoes, picks up his attaché case filled with documents, and heads out.

No one knows where he goes, but we believe he goes to a park or to Starbucks and just hang out for the day, then in the evenings, when he enters the lobby on his way up to his apartment, with the perpetual smile on his face, he would begin speaking about the challenging day he had at the office.

Of late he has been speaking about a new company he has formed and others he's about to launch; he speaks of how well his new company is doing and problems encountered in his effort to launch the others. In his mind, he is the CEO and CFO of those imaginary enterprises.

In one incident, upon entering the lobby late in the evening after a long day at his imaginary office, cheerfully smiling as usual, his suitcase accidentally popped opened while he was still clutching the handle with the case at his side; the contents fell out and was scattered all around him on the floor. he contents were only papers and a zip lock plastic bag which contained a piece of bread, I immediately jumped up in an effort to help in getting his stuff back together.

He immediately responded to my help by saying, "No, please don't. I got it" as he scrambled around gathering the papers as quickly as he could, but from looking down at the sheets of papers, I could see that they were all blank. Not a single word was either written or printed on them. With his fixed smile he said, "Thanks anyway" as he stuffed them in the case and hastily scampered away.

Later that evening, another resident of the building told us that she saw Humphrey today in the park, she observed as he spent hours moving from bench to bench, breaking bread into crumbs and feeding the pigeons with it.

A few months after that incident, we eventually found out through someone who knew him quite well that Humphrey has had an obsession with corporations and their culture since his teen years. He had tried numerous times to gain employment into well-known companies, the mainstream giants. But for one reason or another, without success, save the time he was given a job by one of them to work in their mailroom, but that did not work out very well for him.

He was fired two months to the day after he was hired, terminated because in his position as mail clerk, he would put on a show as if he was the chief executive. He went around asking questions and for information that were not pertinent to his job description. He would contradict and try to correct other seasoned employees, who were engaged in projects vital to the company.

His penchant for the corporate world was uncontrollable to the point where in this humble position, his eagerness to climb the ladder led him to another point where he just about fell short of giving orders. All of this didn't sit well with the other employees, so with many complaints about his uninvited and unwanted impositions, he had to be let go.

Thereafter, he was employed in several temporary jobs in which he brought along the same behavior and, in all cases, had to be terminated. All those terminations did not in the least faze him. In his mind, he was saying to himself, "What do they know anyway?"

In his imaginary corporate world, he was the CEO of CEOs—shrewd, knowledgeable, and ruthless when necessary; it was this self-confidence that kept him happy, this fantasy that kept him always smiling. Knowing about his made-up fantasy world, most of us would consider him just another nutcase, a perfect example of a flake, and we might say, "How can someone who lives in a totally unproductive world of fantasy be so perpetually happy?" But on the other side of the coin, what we should stop to contemplate is, how is it that the rest of us get up each day and go to our real world productive jobs, yet we are mostly unhappy?

We wish to discover what to believe in and why we believe in it; and why such a belief is reasonable, and in so far as possible, enter into the nature of the invisible cause of this manifest life of ours. We wish to discover how this cause works our relationship to it, its relationship to us and how we may use this knowledge.

—Anonymous

We must become bigger than we have been; more courageous, greater in spirit, larger in outlook.

We must become members of a new race, overcoming petty prejudice, owing our ultimate allegiance not to nations, but to our fellowmen within the human community.

—Haile Selassie 1

EPILOGUE

The various individuals observed in this high-rise are merely slices off the big loaf of life. Each slice soaks up whatever environment in which they either find themselves, chose to be in, or thrust into. In these environments, personalities are formed, which in turn produces the characters we become.

About a decade ago, I met a man who had given up on life. He was a middle-aged man who had tried to succeed in all aspects of his life—financially, socially, and romantically—but had failed miserably in all of them. The day I met him he was sitting alone under and in the shade of a huge oak tree. On his face I saw the look of dejection, disappointment, and frustration. In a sensitive manner, I slowly approached him and asked if he was okay and if there was anything that I could do for him.

He looked up at me, thanked me, and said, "I guess I will be OK, but I will say to you this world has become a monetary world, and if you happen to be one of those who have no money, then nobody has any desire to be bothered with you."

As he continued, I could not help but notice the wedding band on his finger. When he saw me gazing at the ring, he anticipated what I was about to ask. Then he said, "In this society, there are two types of men who gets married, a rich man and a fool." And in an elevated tone, he said, "And I am not rich."

We continued talking for about another hour as I tried to cheer him up with positive words and as I spoke, he nodded his head as he thanked me for my kind and uplifting words. As I bade him farewell and turned to walk away, he uttered, "I will also tell you that good people are very hard to find. In order to find one, you will have to search long and hard."

I acknowledged and understood that, in his own world, his statement seemed plausible and resonated with some degree of truth. At that point, I tried to instill in him that when all is said and done, there are still good people out there, and among us, and even though it seems that we are becoming more and more impersonal due to our technological advancements and fast-paced lifestyles, there is still some degree of beauty and simplicity in this world, which makes life still hopeful and worthwhile. He thanked me again as we parted ways.

The characters found in this high-rise, as well as the frustrated man at the big oak, are everywhere and all around. They can be found in friends, relatives, coworkers, and neighbors. They are all of us.

And time marches on.

ABOUT THE AUTHOR

The author is also a fine artist (painter and former art instructor) who, from an early age, has been a keen observer of people and their lifestyles and behaviors, including his own.

Sitting on a park bench, at an outdoor café, or any busy public space, watching the expressions on the faces of passersby is one of his favorite pastime, and to him, it is another form of reading.

Curiosity, among other things, led him to the job as a doorman, which offered further insight into the various roles we all play in this journey called life.

www.ingramcontent.com/pod-product-compliance
Lightning Source LLC
Chambersburg PA
CBHW051059250726
48656CB00001B/370